G000123664

VIVEKANANDA: EAST MEETS WEST

VIVEKANANDA: EAST MEETS WEST

(A Pictorial Biography)

Swami Chetanananda

Preface by Huston Smith

Biographical Introduction by
Christopher Isherwood

VEDANTA SOCIETY OF ST. LOUIS

Printed and bound in the United States of America
First Edition 1995

Library of Congress Cataloging-in-Publication Data

Chetanananda, Swami.
Vivekananda : East meets West : a pictorial biography / Swami Chetanananda ; preface by Huston Smith ; biographical introduction by Christopher Isherwood. — 1st ed.
p. cm.
Includes bibliographical references.
ISBN 0-916356-78-7
1. Vivekananda, Swami, 1863-1902. I. Title.
BL1280.292.V58C486 1994
294.5'55'092 — dc20
[B] 94-45710
CIP

Those who wish to learn in greater detail about the teachings contained in this book may write to: Secretary, Vedanta Society of St. Louis, 205 South Skinker Boulevard, St. Louis, Missouri 63105, U.S.A.

Table of Contents

If I were asked under what sky the human mind has most fully developed some of its choicest gifts, has most deeply pondered on the greatest problems of life, and has found solutions of some of them which well deserve the attention even of those who have studied Plato and Kant — I should point to India.

Max Müller in ***India: What Can It Teach Us?*** (London: 1892)

Preface

In subtitling this new and winning portrait of Vivekananda "East Meets West" Swami Chetanananda is of course accurate, but he modestly understates his case. Spiritually speaking, Vivekananda's words and presence at the 1893 World Parliament of Religions brought Asia to the West decisively. For, reading correctly the spiritual hunger of the West that his words and presence brought to the surface, Vivekananda went on to found the Ramakrishna Mission whose centres in almost every major city of Europe and America launched the influx of Asian spirituality that has changed the religious complexion of those continents permanently. Buddhism, Sufism, Sikhism, Baha'i and others have followed, but Vedanta was the pioneer.

The importance of this fact needs no belabouring, but I should like to expand the notion of East meeting West by pointing out that it houses a temporal as well as a spatial dimension. For though we have no time machine to set clocks back, it *is* possible (in our Westernizing world) to break out of our modern time frame by venturing abroad. When I find Vivekananda reporting that

> when my Master [Sri Ramakrishna] touched me, my mind underwent a complete revolution; I was aghast to realize that there really was nothing whatever in the entire universe but God,

and when he proceeds from such reports to conclude that our seeming self is not our true self, the latter being in actuality divine, I hear his words echoing not only from a different land (India) but from a different time — a past when the human outlook was less hobbled by the materialistic, reductionistic styles of thought that the West has fallen into.

I grant that there is danger in stating things this way, for the cult of novelty has led many people to confuse "past" with "inferior." Reflective thinkers, though, are coming to recognize that on the most important question of life — who are we? where did we come from? what are we supposed to do, if anything? — modern science has confused us, along with clarifying things in other respects. For in being able to deal only with things that are woven of space, time, and matter — things that readers of this book will recognize as pertaining to *maya* (unreality) — science has unwittingly led many people to assume that *samsara* (the relative world) is more important and real than *nirvana* (the experience of absolute Reality).

Personally, therefore, I welcome Vivekananda as an envoy, not only from a different land but from a time that was more open to "the breath of the eternal" that the Upanishads attest to so compellingly. For reminding me of his life and message, told this time in living colour, I am deeply grateful to the author of this book. In saying this I am sure that I speak not only for myself but prolepticly for the countless other readers that I expect his book to have.

Huston Smith

Author's Note

Human life is not eternal, but one who lives completely for others lives forever in the memory of humankind. In one sense, memory is deathless: it rolls successively from one mind to the other. Buddha, Christ, and other great teachers of the world have gone, but they are still alive in the memories of millions and even now are inspiring them. When we read about these great souls, we want to visualize them, because visualization makes a thing more tangible and vivid to us. There is a Chinese proverb: "One picture is worth more than ten thousand words."

One hundred years have passed since Vivekananda came to America to represent Hinduism, or Vedanta, at the Parliament of Religions in Chicago. The purpose of *Vivekananda: East Meets West* is to pay homage to that great swami and to commemorate that historical event. There are 275 photographs in this book, including all available photographs of Vivekananda; the rest are the places and persons connected with his life. He travelled extensively around the world and met many prominent people in the East and the West. In this pictorial I have tried to depict his life and message through the published accounts of his experiences, biographical and autobiographical anecdotes, his letters and lectures, and the reminiscences of his disciples and friends. In fact, this book contains the highlights of those accounts of Vivekananda's glorious and eventful life. With the exception of the introduction to each chapter, all material has been quoted from other sources, some of which I edited for the sake of readability and continuity.

Vivekananda's overwhelming love for and dedication to humanity made him immortal. Once he expressed his passionate love for the ideal: "One eye shed tears of grief when I left home, because I hated to leave my mother, grandmother, brothers and sisters; and the other eye shed tears of joy for my ideal." Like Buddha, Vivekananda sacrificed his life for the good of many and for the welfare of all.

He started his mission at the age of 30 and died at 39. It is really amazing how much he accomplished in this short time. Towards the end of his life he said, "What does it matter! I have given them enough for fifteen hundred years."

Thousands of years ago the Vedanta philosophy avowed "unity in diversity." People of the East and the West are different: their languages, cultures, customs, colours, and religious beliefs all differ. At the same time human consciousness, human nature, and the aspiration for freedom are always the same: many great thinkers of the world have dreamt of and taught this essential unity. Vivekananda experienced that ancient Vedantic truth "unity in diversity"; as a result, his life became the meeting point of the ancient and the modern, the East and the West. Romain Rolland, the great French writer, concluded his famous book *The Life of Vivekananda* with this message: "My European companions, I have made you listen through the Wall, to the blows of the coming one, Asia. . . . Go to meet her! She is working for us. We are working for her. Europe and Asia are the two halves of the Soul. Man *is not* yet. He *will be*."

My heartfelt gratitude goes to Christopher Isherwood, who wrote a biographical sketch based on one of his lectures and sent it to me a few months before his death in January 1986. This biographical account is a fitting introduction to this pictorial on Vivekananda. My special thanks go to Dr. Huston Smith for his thoughtful preface. I am indebted to Marie Louise Burke (Gargi) for allowing me to use some precious photographs from her collection. I am also grateful to the Vedanta students who helped edit, design, and type the manuscript of this book. I am indebted to the friends and members of the Vedanta Society who financially helped this project.

Once Swami Vivekananda blessed a disciple with these words: "I have given you advice enough; now put at least something in practice. Let the world see that your listening to me has been a success."

Chetanananda

St. Louis, Missouri, U.S.A.
11 September 1993

Biographical Introduction*

Although the basic facts about the life and career of Narendranath Datta – later Swami Vivekananda – are fairly well-known, I will begin by running through them very briefly.

He was born on 12 January 1863. He met Sri Ramakrishna when he was 18 and was with him until Ramakrishna's death in 1886. By this time, he had become the natural leader of the young disciples of Sri Ramakrishna, and on Christmas Eve, 1886, these disciples vowed that they would become monks. In 1887 they took the formal vows and assumed monastic names. These names were mostly given to them by Vivekananda himself, and some of them refer to some remarks which Ramakrishna had made about that particular individual.

After the passing away of Sri Ramakrishna, there was a period during which the boys gathered together in an old house at Baranagore. This was their first Math, or monastery. At that time also, they went on long pilgrimages all over India. It was during this period from 1887 to 1893 that Narendranath, now known under various monastic names (actually, Vivekananda was the third name he assumed), wandered all over India. It was during these wanderings that he learned the actual conditions of Indian life, and saw with his own eyes the terrible poverty, squalor, and ignorance in which the masses were living. He also learned to appreciate their extraordinary potential as human beings. It was then that he was filled with the missionary ardor which made him determined to accomplish a great economic, educational, psychological, and spiritual revolution in India.

Then in 1893 he got the opportunity to go to the United States and take part unofficially in the Parliament of Religions which was being held in Chicago. This Parliament of Religions, although it was accompanied by a great deal of grandiose verbiage and eloquence that in some cases make us smile nowadays, was nevertheless one of the most important events in cultural history. It was an extraordinary act of liberalism, and it was effective beyond the founders' wildest dreams, very largely because they had the incredible good luck to have Vivekananda come to it. However, all honour must be given to everybody who had anything to do with the organization of it.

Vivekananda came to Chicago and his natural powers as a speaker made an extraordinary impression. For the next four years, he was in the United States, lecturing, founding groups of students, and finally establishing a centre in New York. He then went to England and returned by way of Europe to India in 1897. That year he and his brother monks got together and formally founded the Ramakrishna Mission. The land was acquired and the plans were made for the future buildings on the spot where the centre of the Math and Mission now stands. The centre, Belur Math, is located on the Ganges outside of Calcutta, not very far along the river from the Dakshineswar temple where Ramakrishna spent almost all of his adult life.

In 1899 Vivekananda came back to the United States by way of Europe and England and was in California where he spent six weeks at a house in Pasadena, which now belongs to the Vedanta Society of Southern California. We can visit it and see the room in which Vivekananda lived, very much as it was at that time.

In 1900 he returned to India already a very sick man, worn out by all the work and the travelling he had done and the hardships he had experienced in his earlier life. On 4 July 1902 he left his body. His death is widely believed to have been voluntary, as we know death can be in certain individuals. Vivekananda was in fact not at all unwell that day. He ate a hearty meal, went for a walk, had long discussions with his brother

Christopher Isherwood wrote this biographical sketch based on one of his lectures.

monks, and then retired for meditation, saying that he did not wish to be disturbed. He then passed into samadhi, and life left the body. Looking back over the weeks that had preceded this, it becomes evident that Vivekananda had been systematically freeing himself from his duties at the Belur Math and preparing others to take them over, and in every way getting ready to lay down his responsibilities and to pass on.

Now this is the brief story of the life of this individual, Vivekananda. Of course, the most important thing about it for us is his encounter with Sri Ramakrishna. George Orwell, in his essay on Gandhi, says that "saints should always be judged guilty until they are proved innocent." This is a sentiment that Ramakrishna himself would have entirely agreed with. He said to his disciples: "You should ring me as the money changer rings a coin to know if it is genuine or not. One should watch one's guru by day and by night. If one has suspicions of him, one should follow them through and make certain that they are either correct or incorrect." Ramakrishna invited this suspicion because he wished to be tested; because he wished his disciples to know that his message had the truth of a true life, of a true spiritual voice.

Among Vivekananda's many tremendous qualities, one of the greatest that he had, for us, was his capacity to be a doubter. Vivekananda was sent to college, like all young men at that time who had had a fairly well-to-do background. Indeed, during his lifetime, Vivekananda's father seemed to be rich; however, it was discovered after his death that he was bankrupt. Vivekananda's education had been Western rather than Indian, since the British were then in command not only militarily and economically, but also to a large extent ideologically, particularly in the large cities such as Calcutta.

So here is this young man — possessed of a powerful body, athletic, a very powerful intelligence, a wide schooling in philosophy, and a considerable knowledge of the ideas of the West — and this boy feels restless without a goal. He wanted to find a meaning in life. He did not find it in the philosophers that the English had brought to India. He did not find it in the indigenous Brahmo Samaj movement, which seemed to him to be lacking in real spiritual inspiration. He was looking, looking for somebody who could inspire him. He was looking for a cause to dedicate his life to. In some respects he reminds one of T. E. Lawrence, Lawrence of Arabia, who in his early years also went through all kinds of austerities, which were not connected in fact with religion at all, but just with a desire to school himself, to strengthen his will, and to accustom his body to obey him throughout fastings and vigils in order that he should be ready for some great emergency. Lawrence, unfortunately, did not find a cause that proved rewarding to his devotion.

But Vivekananda's self-dedication ended in the greatest conceivable triumph. He met Ramakrishna, and was brought to Dakshineswar where already this strange man was being talked about. Ramakrishna had many adherents, and many visitors came to see him out of mere curiosity. He was very strange. He seemed half a baby. He was so unselfconscious that he would let his wearing cloth fall from him and walk about naked. Many times each day he would go into a state of spiritual absorption [samadhi] in which he lost outward consciousness. Then again, he would suddenly bring himself down to the sphere of ordinary sense-perception and talk in a very homely, sensible, familiar way, using a country dialect which was crudely frank, according to the standards of politely educated people, to describe his intimate and constant relationship with the Unseen. It must have been astounding, the atmosphere in that little room. However one tries to describe it, one always comes back to the word *now, the extraordinary nowness* of the situation, because, of course God is the only fact that is eternally *now*. When we talk about current affairs and the latest news — about the Middle East or about whether a certain actor will marry a certain actress, we are not really talking about *now* because every event in this so-called present has strings attached to it — strings that drag us forward into the future or back into the past. We are either trying to slow down and say, "Oops, be careful, or we'll be in trouble," or "Oh, come on. Hurry up. Let's get the show on the road." Whatever we think about, our whole present life is extremely jittery in this way, and it does not have that eternal moment. But when Ramakrishna talked about God, his words had what Gerald Heard — that great maker of memorable phrases — called "an appalling instantaneity." It was absolutely *now* and there you were in the *nowness*.

So this college boy enters Ramakrishna's room and he sees these people, many of them acting — or overacting — religiously. Some are genuinely impressed, others are making jokes (in whispers). All kinds of people have come in there to observe Ramakrishna. The boy does not know what to make of it at all. Then Ramakrishna takes him outside. The room where he lives is not very big and it has porches on either side. Ramakrishna takes him out onto the porch at the back. He says: "At last you have come to me! I know who you are. You are the Lord Nara." Vivekananda is horrified! He thinks: "Well, this man is mad, absolutely crazy. What is all this?" Ramakrishna bows down to him, and then goes back into the room. Vivekananda is deeply disturbed and thinks, "Well, perhaps I had better leave." He comes back into the room later, however — he could not resist — and finds Ramakrishna talking and laughing as though nothing had happened, seeming to be the most sensible of people, and answering with the most absolute simplicity all kinds of abstruse philosophical questions from pundits. He always brought everything right down to earth and was so amusing and sensible and funny. Well, Vivekananda was fascinated. He was hooked. He could not resist Ramakrishna.

Then, of course, there were other great moments. There was the time when Ramakrishna suddenly touched him and Vivekananda had the experience which the Buddhists call "the clear light of the void." The whole of reality vanished into a great whirlpool and he felt that his identity, that everything that belonged to him, was falling away. He was not in the room, and he was not anywhere. He was engulfed. He cried out to Ramakrishna: "What are you doing to me? I have got my parents at home." Ramakrishna laughed and touched him again, saying, "It is all right; it is all over."

Then there was another very strange scene that took place. Vivekananda was always on the lookout for any kind of hypnotism or any attempt to subdue his will by somebody else's will. Since he had, of course, a terrific will, he was quite sure that nobody could ever hypnotize him — certainly not this absurd man who seemed so strange and gentle and loving, enormously loving. Yet one day Ramakrishna did put him into a kind of trance. Vivekananda could not afterwards remember what he had said, but Ramakrishna said to others, "I talked to him and he told me who he was"; he seems to have meant that these two beings, whatever you want to call them, who had temporarily incarnated in the forms of this strange, eccentric priest and this college student, had some kind of eternal association, and had made a rendezvous, as it were, to meet at this particular point in time.

After that, Vivekananda was indeed a faithful disciple for the rest of his life. But even then his doubts persisted and only gradually, gradually disappeared. A lot of us, reading *The Gospel of Sri Ramakrishna*, perhaps think: "Well he is really being very tiresome. Heavens, if I had met Ramakrishna I would have got his number in a minute. I would have said, 'Oh, that is God.' I would have bowed down and my doubts would have disappeared." But Vivekananda's doubt was the very measure of Vivekananda's greatness. If I meet somebody and say, "All right, he is a saint. I believe," the heavens do not fall. It does not change my life. But when a being like Vivekananda is converted, then the whole of the nineteenth century is altered. One cannot sufficiently stress that point, that a great man has great doubts and a great conversion and that there are tremendous effects from that conversion.

Now, of course, there is another aspect of Vivekananda's life, and that is his mission to the West, something that can hardly be discussed in this short introduction. But what was basically so great about Vivekananda was that his coming to the West — and, of course, his subsequent return to India, then again to the West and again back to India — had such a wonderful balance. In other words, he was not just arriving from India to say, "Now, all you sinners out here in America, you are all going to be converted, and the cure for everything is Ramakrishna." As a matter of fact, he hardly preached directly about Ramakrishna at all. To the West he said: "Yes, you are hopelessly materialistic. It is disgusting, the way you are enslaved by money, fame and power." He taught them that India was an extremely spiritual country, and that they should not look down on India simply because India had been invaded and conquered, and because India had not got the same technological standards that America had.

On the other hand, he returned to India and told them, "My goodness! If you had some of the energy that they have in the West, then maybe you would get somewhere." "You cannot manufacture a pin, and you dare to criticize the English," he said on one occasion. You see, in other words, he balanced the whole thing, and what he was really crusading for was an interchange of what the East had to give to the West and what the West had to give to the East. That was the whole meaning of his mission.

Towards the end of his life, after this tremendous activity, after all this fury and fun and energy, after all his speeches, after all his battles against various obstacles and opponents, he became very calm. There are, of course, two kinds of calm, and it is as though in the middle of life there is the one great raging river of energy which is called *rajas*, the power which not only destroys a lot of things, but also creates a lot of things, gets a lot of things done. Vivekananda had plunged boldly into that river. Now he reached its further bank.

It is worth saying a word about the kind of calm that comes over a man of this sort because it is so very often misrepresented. We hear so much about Oriental religions being so passive, and how they are always just mooning and sitting around being lazy. The most polar opposition in life is between the inertia of sloth and the calm of a great saint who in the end can say and really mean it, "In His will is our peace." The saint is on the further bank of the river. On the closest bank you get the winos of skid row. Both of them seem actionless, but in a different way. Whereas the winos only end up finding the Salvation Army — which is certainly a very good thing to find, but nevertheless all they can hope for in the immediate future — the saints are in the *now*, the appalling instantaneity.

I always feel that, talking about Vivekananda, one has to end by letting him speak for himself. Everything he said or wrote was characteristic of what he was, no matter whether he was joking or deeply in earnest. Here are a few extracts from his talks and letters:

"The whole world is a succession of dreams. My ambition is to be a conscious dreamer."

"Do not work yourself out. It is no use; always remember — 'Duty is the midday sun whose fierce rays are burning the very vitals of humanity.' It is necessary for a time as a discipline; beyond that, it is a morbid dream. Things go on all right whether we lend them our helping hands or not. We in delusion only break ourselves. There is a false sentiment which goes to the extreme of unselfishness, 'only to injure others by its submission to every evil.' We have no right to make others selfish by our unselfishness; have we?"

"This toy world would not be here, this play could not go on, if we were knowing players. We must play blindfolded. Some of us have taken the part of the rogue of the play, some heroic. Never mind, it is all play. This is the only consolation. There are demons and lions and tigers and what not on the stage, but they are all muzzled. They snap but cannot bite. The world cannot touch our souls. If you want, even if the body be torn and bleeding, you may enjoy the greatest peace in your mind.

"And the way to that is to attain hopelessness.... Not the imbecile attitude of despair, but the contempt of the conqueror for things he has attained. . . .

"This hopelessness, desirelessness, aimlessness, is just the harmony with nature. In nature there is no harmony, no reason, no sequence; it was chaos before, it is so still.

"The lowest man is in consonance with nature in his earthy-headness; the highest the same in the fullness of knowledge. All three aimless, drifting, hopeless — all three happy."

"If living by rule alone ensures excellence, if it be virtue strictly to follow the rules and customs handed down through generations, say then, who is more virtuous than a tree? Who is a greater devotee, a holier saint, than a railway train?"

"Let the barks of puppies not frighten you. No, not even the thunderbolts of heaven, but stand up and work!"

"I love the Yankee land. I like to see new things. I do not care a fig to loaf about old ruins and mope a life out about old histories and keep singing about the ancients. I have too much vigor in my blood for that. In America is the place, the people, the opportunity for everything new."

"No harm to the world in my being happy and being miserable, but others must not catch it. This is the great fact. No sooner does a prophet feel miserable for the state of man than he sours his face, beats his breast, and calls upon everyone to drink tartaric acid and munch charcoal and sit upon a dung-heap covered with ashes and speak only in groans and tears! I find they all have been wanting. Yes, they have. If you are really ready to take up the earth's burden, take it up by all means — but do not let us hear your groans and curses. Do not frighten us with your sufferings, so that we come to feel we were better off with our own burden. The man who really takes up the burden blesses the world and goes his own way. He has not a word of condemnation, not a word of criticism — not because there was no evil, but because he has taken it on his own shoulders willingly, voluntarily. It is the Saviour who should go on his way rejoicing — and not the saved."

"No country on earth [the United States] has so many laws and in no country are they so little regarded. On the whole, our poor Hindu people are infinitely more moral than any of the Westerns. In religion they practise either hypocrisy or fanaticism."

"The Germans are constructing after the French fashion, big houses and mansions and placing big statues, equestrian figures, etc. on top of them. But on seeing a double-storied German building, one is tempted to ask, 'Is it a dwelling house for men, or a stable for elephants and camels?' While, at the same time, one mistakes a five-storied French stable for elephants and horses as a habitation for fairies."

"Look here. We shall all die. Bear this in mind always and then the spirit within will wake up. Then only meanness will vanish from you. Practicality and work will come and you will get new vigor in mind and body. And those who come in contact with you will also feel that they have really got something uplifting from you. Then you will see that the constant thought of death is giving you new life."

And then, to end up with, this famous letter that I think one can never read often enough, which he wrote to the lady he called "Joe," Josephine MacLeod, right at the end of his life: "After all, Joe, I am only the boy who used to listen with rapt wonderment to the wonderful words of Ramakrishna under the banyan at Dakshineswar. That is my true nature — works and activities, doing good and so forth, are all superimpositions. Now I again hear his voice, the same old voice thrilling my soul. Bonds are breaking — love dying, work becoming tasteless — the glamour is off life. Now only the voice of the Master calling. — 'I come, Lord, I come.' . . .

"I am glad I was born, glad I suffered so, glad I did make big blunders, glad to enter peace. I leave none bound, I take no bonds. Whether this body will fall and release me or I enter into freedom in the body, the old man is gone, gone forever, never to come back again! The guide, the guru, the leader, the teacher has passed away; the boy, the student, the servant, is left behind. . . .

"The sweetest moments of my life have been when I was drifting. I am drifting again — with the bright warm sun ahead and masses of vegetation around — and in the heat everything is so still, so calm — and I am drifting languidly in the warm heart of the river! I dare not make a splash with my hands or feet — for fear of breaking the marvellous stillness, stillness that makes you feel sure it is an illusion!

"Behind my work was ambition, behind my love was personality, behind my purity was fear, behind my guidance the thirst of power! Now they are vanishing, and I drift. I come! Mother, I come! In Thy warm bosom, floating wheresoever Thou takest me, in the voiceless, in the strange, in the wonderland, I come — a spectator, no more an actor.

"Oh, it is so calm! My thoughts seem to come from a great, great distance in the interior of my own heart. They seem like faint, distant whispers, and peace is upon everything, sweet, sweet peace — like that one feels for a few moments just before falling into sleep, when things are seen and felt like shadows — without fear, without love, without emotion. Peace that one feels alone, surrounded with statues and pictures — I come! Lord, I come!"

Christopher Isherwood

I

Narendra – "Chief of Men"

Swami Vivekananda was born in Calcutta on 12 January 1863, and was given the name Narendra Nath Datta. Many years later he wrote to an American devotee about his premonastic name: "It is a very poetic name. Narendra means the 'Chief of men' (nara means man, and indra stands for ruler or chief). Very ludicrous, isn't it? But such are the names in our country; we cannot help it, but I am glad that I have given that up." It is a custom in India for a monk to renounce his name and all other attachments, so that he can be absorbed in Brahman.

Narendra, or Naren, was a precocious boy — very truthful and idealistic. His innate tendency towards meditation was evident even in his early life: meditation was one of his childhood games.

His father, Vishwanath Datta, was an attorney of the Calcutta High Court. He was extremely generous and had a progressive outlook in social and religious matters, owing perhaps to the influence of Western culture. Narendra's mother, Bhuvaneshwari Devi, was deeply religious. She raised her children according to the ancient spiritual tradition of India and taught Narendra: "Remain pure all your life; guard your own honour and never transgress the honour of others. Be very tranquil, but when necessary, harden your heart."

Brought up and educated in nineteenth-century Calcutta, Narendra was introduced at an early age to the principles of Western thinking, one of which was that one should not accept anything without evidence. Although he was a brilliant student and was well-versed in history, philosophy, literature, and contemporary Western thought, he held firmly to the idea: "Do not believe a thing because you read it in a book. Do not believe a thing because another has said it is so. Find out the truth for yourself. That is realization."

His college principal, William Hastie, said about him: "Narendranath is really a genius. I have travelled far and wide but I have never yet come across a lad of his talents and possibilities, even in German universities, amongst philosophical students."

Narendra was gifted in many ways: he was a musician, debater, gymnast, and philanthropist. He was energy personified. Later, he told one of his English disciples: "In my childhood I used to observe an inexhaustible force arising in me, overflowing my body, as it were. I used to become restless and could not keep quiet. This was why I used to fidget all the time. . . . My insides would vibrate, as it were, and make me restless to do something."

Romain Rolland wrote in his biography of Vivekananda: "He was tall (five feet, eight and a half inches; 170 pounds), square-shouldered, broad-chested, stout, rather heavily built; his arms were muscular and trained to all kinds of sports. He had an olive complexion, a full face, vast forehead, strong jaw, a pair of magnificent eyes, large, dark and rather prominent, with heavy lids, whose shape recalled the classic comparison to a lotus petal. Nothing escaped the magic of his glance, capable equally of embracing in its irresistible charm, or of sparkling with wit, irony, or kindness, of losing itself in ecstasy, or of plunging imperiously to the very depths of consciousness and of withering with its fury. But his pre-eminent characteristic was kingliness. He was a born king and nobody ever came near him either in India or America without paying homage to his majesty."

One day I found that my mind was soaring high in samadhi along a luminous path. It soon transcended the stellar universe and entered the subtler region of ideas. As it ascended higher and higher, I found on both sides of the way ideal forms of gods and goddesses. The mind then reached the outer limits of that region, where a luminous barrier separated the sphere of relative existence from that of the Absolute. Crossing that barrier, the mind entered the transcendental realm, where no corporeal being was visible. Even the gods dared not peep into that sublime realm, and were content to keep their seats far below. But the next moment I saw seven venerable sages seated there in samadhi. It occurred to me that these sages must have surpassed not only men but even the gods in knowledge and holiness, in renunciation and love. Lost in admiration, I was reflecting on their greatness, when I saw a portion of that undifferentiated luminous region condense into the form of a divine child. The child came to one of the sages, tenderly clasped his neck with his lovely arms, and addressing him in a sweet voice, tried to drag his mind down from the state of samadhi. That magic touch roused the sage from the superconscious state, and he fixed his half-opened eyes upon the wonderful child. His beaming countenance showed that the child must have been the treasure of his heart. In great joy the strange child spoke to him: "I am going down. You too must go with me." The sage remained mute but his tender look expressed his assent. As he kept gazing at the child, he was again immersed in samadhi. I was surprised to find that a fragment of his body and mind was descending to earth in the form of a bright light. No sooner had I seen Narendra than I recognized him to be that sage. [Sri Ramakrishna later admitted that the divine child who brought about the descent of the sage was none other than himself.]

— *Ramakrishna (1836-1886)*

Ramakrishna in samadhi (Calcutta, 21 September 1879)

Varanasi, the City of Light, from the Ganges

Bhuvaneshwari Devi [Narendra's mother] wrote to an old aunt of the Datta family in Varanasi, asking her to make the necessary offerings and prayers to Vireshwar Shiva that a son might be born to her. It was arranged that on Mondays the aunt would offer worship to Vireshwar Shiva, while Bhuvaneshwari would practise special austerities on those days. It is said that by observing a vow of this sort for one year, one is blessed with a son. Thus Bhuvaneswari was content to wait in perfect assurance that her prayers would be answered. She spent her days in practising japa and meditation. She observed fasts and intensified her many other austerities, her whole soul given over to constant recollectedness, her heart fixed in love on the Lord Shiva.

One night Bhuvaneshwari had a vivid dream. She saw the Lord Shiva rouse himself from his meditation and take the form of a male child who was to be her son. She awoke. Could this ocean of light in which she found herself bathed be but a dream? Shiva! Shiva!

The light of the world dawned for the first time upon the future Swami Vivekananda on Monday, 12 January 1863.

Vireshwar Shiva, Varanasi

Bhuvaneshwari Devi (1841-1911), below: her signature

You went to see my poor mother and brothers. I am glad you did. But you have touched the only soft place in my heart. You ought to know, Diwanji [Haridas Viharidas Desai], that I am no hard-hearted brute. If there is any being I love in the whole world, it is my mother. Yet I believed and still believe that without my giving up the world, the great mission which Ramakrishna Paramahamsa, my great Master, came to preach would not see the light.

The mother is the God in our family. The idea is that the only real love that we see in the world, the most unselfish love, is in the mother; always suffering, always loving; and what love can represent the love of God more than the love which we see in the mother? Thus the mother is the type, the incarnation of God on earth to the Hindu. . . . The love which my mother gave to me has made me what I am, and I owe a debt to her that I can never repay.

— *Vivekananda*

Every night [as a boy] when I went to bed, two ideals of life appeared before me. One of them was to be a man of great wealth, surrounded by servants and dependents and enjoying high rank and immense power. I saw myself as foremost among the great men of the world; and I certainly had the necessary ability in me to fulfill that ambition. But then, the very next moment, I would picture myself as having renounced everything in the world. I was wearing nothing but a loincloth, eating without anxiety whatever food came my way, sleeping under a tree and living in complete reliance on God's will. I knew it was within me to lead this life of the sages and ascetics, if I should choose to do so. These two pictures of the two directions in which I could bend my life kept appearing before me; but I always ended by choosing the latter. I knew that this was the only path by which a man could achieve true happiness, and I resolved to follow it and not the other. As I dwelt on the happiness of such a life, my mind would become absorbed in God and I would fall asleep.

— *Vivekananda*

Two mendicants of the Himalayas

Vivekananda's ancestral house (foreground), 3 Gour Mohan Mukherjee Lane, Calcutta

Calcutta, ca. 1886

Sunrise at Calcutta on the Ganges

From the earliest times that I can remember, I used to see a marvellous point of light between my eyebrows as soon as I shut my eyes to go to sleep, and I used to watch its various changes with great attention. In order to watch it better, I'd kneel on the bed in the attitude a devotee takes when he prostrates before a shrine, his forehead touching the ground. That marvellous point of light would change colours and get bigger and bigger until it took the form of a ball; finally it would burst and cover my body from head to foot with white liquid light. As soon as that happened, I would lose outer consciousness and fall asleep. I used to believe that that was the way everybody went to sleep. Then, when I grew older and began to practise meditation, that point of light would appear to me as soon as I closed my eyes, and I'd concentrate upon it. At that time, I was practising meditation with a few friends, following the instructions of Devendra Nath Tagore. We told each other about the visions and experiences we had had. And that was how I found out that none of them had ever seen that point of light or gone to sleep in that way.

— *Vivekananda*

WE CANNOT QUESTION THAT Sri Ramakrishna recognized such a soul, "a Brahmajnani [knower of Brahman] from his birth," in the lad Naren, when he first saw him; recognized too, like a skilled engineer measuring the force of a stream, the height to which his thought-transcendence had already mounted. "Tell me, do you see a light when you are going to sleep?" asked the old man eagerly. "Doesn't everyone?" answered the boy, in wonder. In later life, he would often mention this question, and digress, to describe to us the light he saw. Sometimes it would come as a ball, which a boy was kicking towards him. It would draw near. He would become one with it, and all would be forgotten. Sometimes it was a blaze, into which he would enter.

— *Sister Nivedita (Margaret Noble, Vivekananda's Irish disciple)*

While at school, one night I was meditating within closed doors and had a fairly deep concentration of mind. How long I meditated in that way, I cannot say. . . . When I kept my mind still and devoid of all objects, there flowed in it a current of serene bliss. Under its influence, I felt a sort of intoxication for a long time even after the end of the meditation; so I did not feel inclined to leave my seat and get up immediately. When I was sitting in that condition at the end of the meditation, I saw the wonderful figure of a monk appear suddenly — from where I did not know — and stand before me at a little distance, filling the room with a divine effulgence. He was in ochre robes with a kamandalu [waterpot] in his hand. His face bore such a calm and serene expression of inwardness born of indifference to all things, that I was amazed and felt much drawn to him. He walked towards me with a slow step, his eyes steadfastly fixed on me, as if he wanted to say something. But I was seized with fear and could not keep still. I got up from my seat, opened the door, and quickly left the room. The next moment I thought, "Why this foolish fear?" I became bold and went back into the room to listen to the monk, who, alas, was no longer there. I waited long in vain, feeling dejected and repenting that I had been so stupid as to flee without listening to him. I have seen many monks, but never have I seen such an extraordinary expression on any other face. That face has been indelibly printed on my heart. It may have been an hallucination; but very often I think that I had the good fortune of seeing Lord Buddha that day.

— *Vivekananda*

Buddha

Vivekananda's study room at his grandmother's residence, 9 Ramtanu Bose Lane, Calcutta

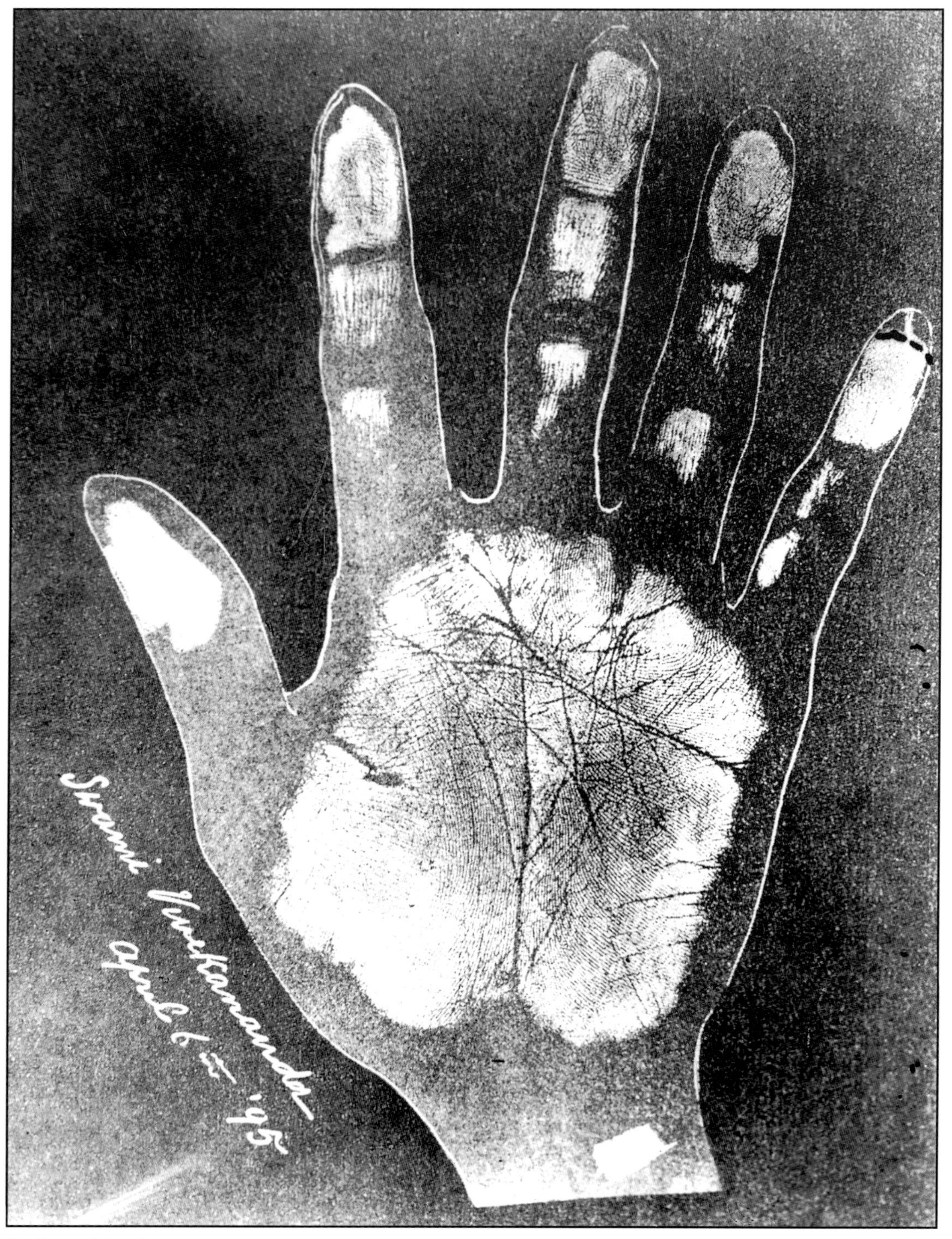

Vivekananda's palm

Naren was a devout admirer of mendicant monks. To see one was a moment of pleasure for him. If the meeting took place at his home, he would anticipate and fulfill the sadhu's needs as far as he could. And the monks always blessed him, for his eyes spoke volumes, and it is in the eyes that the monks see the soul reflected. The longing to be a monk himself was always in Naren. He often thought of the time when he would be free to follow that life. In his boyish fervour he would tell his friends what he would do, where he would go, and so on, enthusing his companions also. Often would he ask a newcomer to the Metropolitan Institution if there was an ancestor in the family, more particularly a grandfather, who had adopted the sannyasin's life. If the reply was positive, Naren would regard the new lad with special favour. Sometimes the boys would get together and in play try, by reading one another's palms, to foretell the future. Naren was the chief palmist of them all. He told them that he would be a monk: there was no mistake about it. "See!" he would say triumphantly, "there is the sure sign of a sannyasin." And he would point out certain lines on his hand which an old man had once told him were characteristic of the tendency to monkhood.

At my birth my father had a horoscope taken of my life, but would never tell me what it was. Some years ago when I visited my home, my father having died, I came across the chart among some papers in my mother's possession and saw from it that I was destined to become a wanderer on the face of the earth.

— *Vivekananda*

Once he [Narendra] said: "Just two or three days before the Entrance examination I found that I hardly knew anything of geometry. So I began to study the subject, keeping awake the whole night, and in twenty-four hours I mastered the four books of geometry."

At this time he acquired a special power of reading which he described as follows: "It so happened that I could understand an author without reading his book line by line. I could get the meaning by just reading the first and the last lines of a paragraph. As this power developed I found it unnecessary to read even the paragraphs. I could follow by reading only the first and last lines of a page. Further, where the author introduced discussions to explain a matter and it took him four or five or even more pages to clear the subject, I could grasp the whole trend of his arguments by only reading the first few lines."

Hearing but a few words of the opponent, he could understand the trend of the arguments in support of the other's position and he would be ready with his reply beforehand. Asked how he could find such fine arguments ever ready to defeat his opponent, he once said: "How many new thoughts are there in the world? If those few thoughts are known together with the reasons for and against them, no necessity for further thinking ever arises, and one is always ready with the replies. For, whatever reason the opponent might adduce in favour of his position, it cannot but be one or the other of those few. Rare indeed are the persons who can give to the world new ideas and thoughts on any subject."

Calcutta, ca. 1886

Dr. Brajendra Nath Seal, a renowned philosopher and vice-chancellor of Mysore University

When I first met Vivekananda in 1881, we were fellow-students of Principal William Hastie, scholar, metaphysician, and poet, at the General Assembly's College. He was my senior in age, though I was his senior in the College by one year. Undeniably a gifted youth, sociable, free and unconventional in manners, a sweet singer, the soul of social circles, a brilliant conversationalist, somewhat bitter and caustic, piercing with the shafts of a keen wit the shows and mummeries of the world, sitting in the scorner's chair but hiding the tenderest of hearts under that garb of cynicism; altogether an inspired Bohemian but possessing what Bohemians lack, an iron will; somewhat preemptory and absolute, speaking with accents of authority and withal possessing a strange power of the eye which could hold his listeners in thrall. . . .

I saw and recognized in him a high, ardent and pure nature, vibrant and resonant with impassioned sensibilities. He was certainly no sour or cross-grained puritan, no normal hypochondriac; he would indulge cynically in unconventional language except when he would spare my innocence. He took an almost morbid delight in shocking conventionality in its tabernacles, respectability in its booths; and in the pursuit of his sport would appear other than he was, puzzling and mystifying those outside his inner circle of friends. But in the recesses of his soul he wrestled with the fierce and fell spirit of Desire, the subtle and illusive spirit of Fancy.

— *Brajendra Nath Seal*

In 1881 Narendra was studying in the General Assembly's Institution. One day, Professor W. W. Hastie, the Principal, was explaining Wordsworth's reference to trance in his poem *The Excursion*. "Such an experience," he said, "is the result of purity of mind and concentration on some particular object, and it is rare indeed, particularly in these days. I have seen only one person who has experienced that blessed state of mind, and he is Ramakrishna Paramahamsa of Dakshineswar. You can understand if you go there and see for yourself." ❧

Principal W. W. Hastie

II

"RAMAKRISHNA – MY MASTER"

In his intense desire to realize the truth, Narendra practised meditation, studied different religious and philosophical systems of the East and the West, and met different religious leaders, but to no avail. Nothing could satisfy his all-devouring hunger for truth. At last he met Sri Ramakrishna at the Dakshineswar temple garden near Calcutta and asked this simple question, "Sir, have you seen God?" Without a moment's hesitation Sri Ramakrishna replied: "Yes, I have seen God. I see him as I see you here, only more clearly. God can be seen. One can talk to him. But who cares for God? People shed torrents of tears for their wives, children, wealth, and property, but who weeps for the vision of God? If one cries sincerely for God, one can surely see him."

"That impressed me at once," said Narendra. "For the first time I found a man who dared to say that he saw God, that religion was a reality, to be felt, to be sensed in an infinitely more intense way than we can sense the world. I began to go to that man, day after day, and I actually saw that religion could be given. One touch, one glance, can change a whole life."

From 1881 to 1886, a close relationship developed between Ramakrishna and Narendra. Narendra's doubts and scepticism were gradually dispelled by Ramakrishna's spiritual power and realizations. Ramakrishna's overwhelming love and concern made Narendra his own forever. He trained Narendra in a number of spiritual disciplines and initiated him into the teachings of nondualistic Vedanta. Narendra also learned from the Master practical Vedanta and how to serve human beings as God.

Narendra's father died in 1884 leaving his family in financial hardship. Although Narendra had graduated from college in 1883, he could not get a job. During this period, he passed through various trials and tribulations, but never lost faith in God. His Master, Ramakrishna, always protected him and guided him.

In the middle of 1885 Ramakrishna contracted throat cancer, but without concern for his body, he continued to train his disciples. When they begged him not to strain himself, he replied: "I do not care. I will give up twenty thousand such bodies to help one man." He distributed monastic robes to Narendra and some of the other young disciples. One day he wrote on a piece of paper, "Naren will teach people." Before his passing away on 16 August 1886, Ramakrishna made Narendra the leader of his group of young disciples. They later formed the Ramakrishna Order.

Ten years later, Narendra (then known as Vivekananda) conveyed his Master's message to humanity: "First make character — that is the highest duty you can perform. Know the truth for yourself, and there will be many to whom you can teach it afterwards; they will all come. He [Ramakrishna] criticized no one. For years I lived with that man, but never did I hear those lips utter one word of condemnation for any sect. I learned from my Master that the religions of the world are not contradictory or antagonistic. They are but various phases of one eternal religion."

The Dakshineswar Temple (founded 1855): Ramakrishna lived and taught here for thirty years.

Humanly speaking, without the temple of Dakshineswar there would have been no Ramakrishna, without Ramakrishna no Vivekananda, and without Vivekananda no Western Mission. The whole story rested on the building, erected on the Ganges side, a few miles above Calcutta, just before the middle of the nineteenth century.

— *Sister Nivedita*

When at a later date, Ramakrishna was asked about Naren's first visit to Dakshineswar [November 1881], he said: "Naren entered the room by the western door, the one that faces the Ganges. I noticed that he had no concern about his bodily appearance; his hair and his clothes weren't tidy at all. He seemed altogether unattached, as if nothing external appealed to him. His eyes showed that the greater part of his mind was turned inward, all of the time. When I saw this, I marvelled to myself, 'How is it possible that such a great spiritual aspirant can live in Calcutta, the home of the worldly-minded?'

"There was a mat spread out on the floor. I asked him to sit, and he sat down near the jar of Ganges water. . . . I asked him to sing. He began singing the Brahmo song:

Oh mind, let us go home —
Why do you roam the world, that foreign land,
And wear its alien garb?"

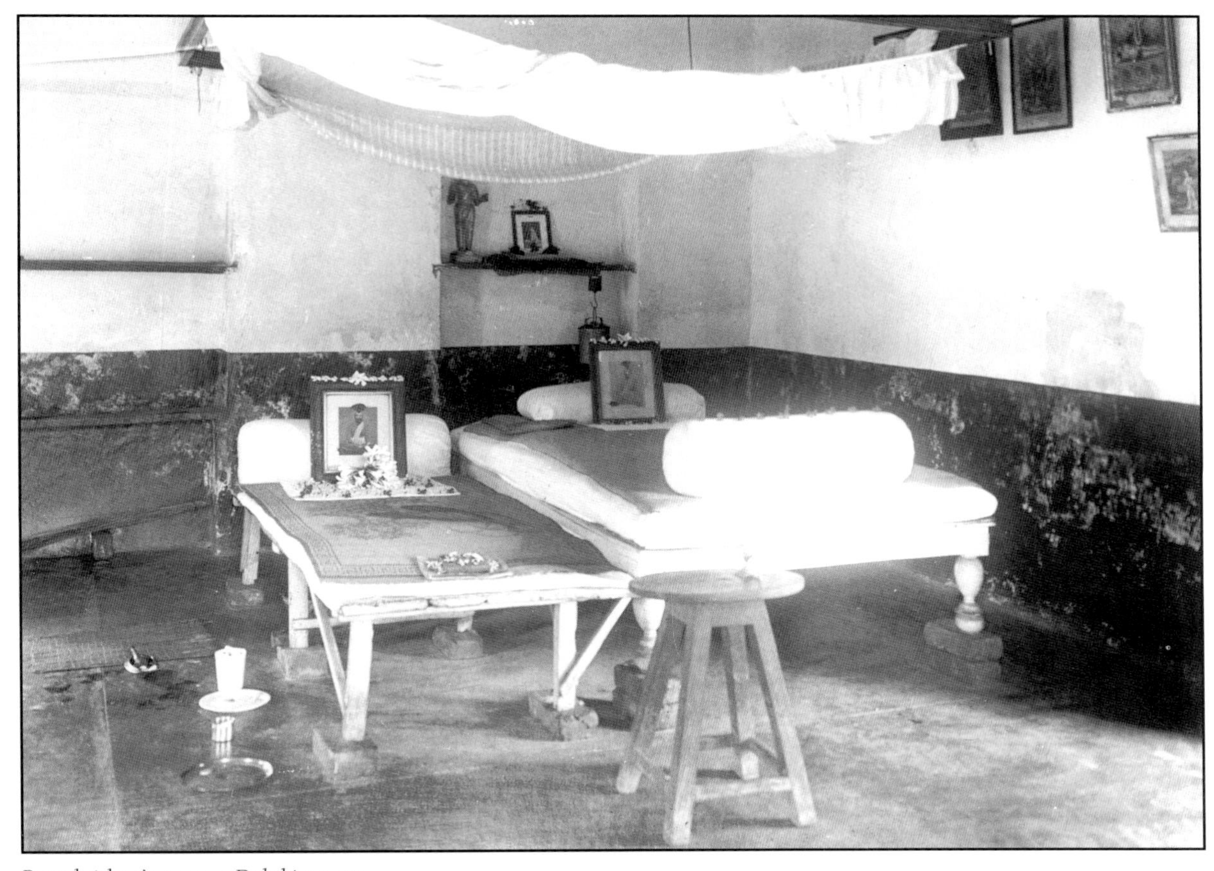

Ramakrishna's room at Dakshineswar

Narendra described the amazing scene which immediately followed:

As soon as I had finished that song, the Master stood up, took me by the hand and led me on to the northern veranda. It was winter, so the open spaces between the pillars were covered with screens of matting to keep out the north wind; and this meant that when the door of the room was closed anyone standing on the veranda was hidden from both inside and outside. As soon as we were on the veranda, the Master closed the door. I thought he must be going to give me some instruction in private. But what he said and did next was something I could never have believed possible. He suddenly caught hold of my hand and began shedding tears of joy. He said to me affectionately as if to a familiar friend: "You've come so late! Was that right? Couldn't you have guessed how I've been waiting for you? My ears are nearly burned off, listening to the talk of these worldly people. I thought I should burst, not having anyone to tell how I really felt!" He went on like that — raving and weeping. And then suddenly he folded his palms together and began addressing me as if I were some divine being: "I know who you are, My Lord. You are Nara, the ancient sage, the incarnation of Narayana. You have come back to earth to take away the sufferings and sorrows of mankind." I was absolutely dumbfounded. I said to myself: "What kind of a man is this? He must be raving mad! How can he talk like this to me, who am nobody — the son of Vishwanath Datta?" But I didn't answer him, and I let this wonderful madman go on talking as he chose. Presently he asked me to stay there on the veranda, and he went back into the room and came out again bringing butter, rock candy, and a few pieces of sandesh; and then he began feeding me with his own hands. I kept asking him to give me the sweetmeats, so I could share them with my friends, but he wouldn't. "They'll get some later," he said, "you take these for yourself." And he wouldn't be satisfied until I'd eaten all of them. Then he took my hand and said, "Promise me — you'll come back here soon, alone." I couldn't refuse his request; it was made so earnestly. So I had to say, "I will." Then I went back into the room with him and sat down beside my friends.

The northern veranda of Ramakrishna's room

Ramakrishna, Dakshineswar, 1884

Regarding his conflicting thoughts about the strange words and conduct of Sri Ramakrishna, Narendra used to say:

I sat and watched him. There was nothing wrong in his words, movements or behaviour towards others. Rather, from his spiritual words and ecstatic states he seemed to be a man of genuine renunciation; and there was a marked consistency between his words and life. He used the most simple language, and I thought, "Can this man be a great teacher?" I crept near him and asked him the question which I had asked so often: "Have you seen God, sir?" "Yes, I see Him just as I see you here, only in a much intenser sense." "God can be realized," he went on. "One can see and talk to Him as I am seeing and talking to you. But who cares? People shed torrents of tears for their wife and children, for wealth or property, but who does so for the sake of God? If one weeps sincerely for Him, He surely manifests Himself." That impressed me at once. For the first time I found a man who dared to say that he had seen God, that religion was a reality to be felt, to be sensed in an infinitely more intense way than we can sense the world. As I heard these things from his lips, I could not but believe that he was saying them not like an ordinary preacher, but from the depths of his own realizations. But I could not reconcile his words with his strange conduct with me. So I concluded that he must be a monomaniac. Yet I could not help acknowledging the magnitude of his renunciation. "He may be a madman," I thought, "but only the fortunate few can have such renunciation. Even if insane, this man is the holiest of the holy, a true saint, and for that alone he deserves the reverent homage of mankind!" With such conflicting thoughts I bowed before him and begged leave to return to Calcutta.

The temple garden of Dakshineswar from the Ganges

Here is Narendra's description of his second visit to Dakshineswar:

I had no idea that the Dakshineswar temple was so far from Calcutta, because I had been there only once before and that was in a carriage. This time, it seemed as if the journey would never end, however far I walked. But, after asking many people the way, I arrived at Dakshineswar at last and went straight to the Master's room. I found him sitting, deep in his own meditations, on the smaller bed which stands beside the bigger one. There was no one with him. As soon as he saw me, he called me joyfully to him and made me sit down on one end of the bed. He was in a strange mood. He muttered something to himself which I couldn't understand, looked hard at me, then rose and approached me. I thought we were about to have another crazy scene. Scarcely had that thought passed through my mind before he placed his right foot on my body. Immediately, I had a wonderful experience. My eyes were wide open, and I saw that everything in the room, including the walls themselves, was whirling rapidly around and receding, and at the same time, it seemed to me that my consciousness of self, together with the entire universe, was about to vanish into a vast, all-devouring void. This destruction of my consciousness of self seemed to me to be the same thing as death. I felt that death was right before me, very close. Unable to control myself, I cried out loudly: "Ah, what are you doing to me? Don't you know I have my parents at home?" When the Master heard this, he gave a loud laugh. Then, touching my chest with his hand, he said: "All right — let it stop now. It needn't be done all at once. It will happen in its own good time." To my amazement, this extraordinary vision of mine vanished as suddenly as it had come. I returned to my normal state and saw things inside and outside the room standing stationary, as before.

When Naren did return [to Dakshineswar], about a week later, he was very much on his guard; determined not to be hypnotized. Ramakrishna proposed that they should walk together in a nearby garden just south of the Dakshineswar compound, because the compound itself happened to be crowded with devotees. They went into the garden house [Jadu Mallick's] — the same in which Ramakrishna had first seen the picture of the Virgin with the child Jesus — and sat down. After a short while, Ramakrishna passed into samadhi. Naren watched him.

Jadu Mallick's garden house, Dakshineswar

Painting of Madonna and child Jesus seen by Ramakrishna (original now in the Vedanta Society of San Francisco)

Suddenly, Ramakrishna touched him, just as on the previous occasion. Despite Naren's strong will to resist, he was unable to cling to his consciousness. This time he became completely unconscious. When he came to himself, he found that Ramakrishna was passing his hand over his chest and smiling at him, sweetly and gently. He had no idea what had happened in the meanwhile.

On a later occasion, Ramakrishna told some of his other disciples: "That day, after Naren had lost consciousness of his present individuality, I asked him many questions — such as who he really was, where he had come from, how long he would stay in this world, and so forth. I made him able to enter into his innermost being and find the answer to my questions there. These answers confirmed what I'd already learned about him in visions. It is forbidden to tell all those things. But I can tell you that, on the day when he knows who he really is, he will no longer remain in this world. With a strong effort of will he will immediately give up his body through the power of yoga. Naren is a great soul, perfect in meditation."

On different occasions Ramakrishna talked about his main disciple Narendra:

Narendra is a boy of a very high order. He excels in everything: vocal and instrumental music and studies. Again, he has control over his sense organs. He is truthful and has discrimination and dispassion. So many virtues in one person!

Well, if Keshab is possessed of one sign of greatness which has made him famous, Naren has eighteen such signs. In Keshab and Vijay I saw the light of knowledge burning like a candle flame, but in Narendra it was like a blazing sun, dispelling the last vestige of ignorance and delusion. . . .

Narendra belongs to a very high plane — the realm of the Absolute. He has a manly nature. So many devotees come here, but there is not one like him.

Every now and then I take stock of devotees. I find that some are like lotuses with ten petals, some like those with sixteen petals, some like those with a hundred petals; but among lotuses Narendra is a thousand-petalled one. Other devotees may be like pots or pitchers; but Narendra is a large water barrel. Others may be like pools or tanks; but Narendra is a huge reservoir like the Haldarpukur. Among fish, Narendra is a huge red-eyed carp; others are like minnows or smelts or sardines. Narendra is a very big receptacle, one that can hold many things. He is like a bamboo with a big hollow space inside.

Narendra is not under the control of anything. He is not under the control of attachment or sense pleasures. He is like a male pigeon. If you hold a male pigeon by its beak, it breaks away from you; but the female pigeon keeps still. Narendra has the nature of a man. . . . I feel great strength when Narendra is with me at a gathering. . . .

Naren is a nitya-siddha, perfect in realization even from his very birth; Naren is a dhyana-siddha, an adept in meditation; the roaring fire of knowledge, always ablaze in Naren, burns to ashes whatever impure food he may take. Impurity of food can never tarnish his pure mind. He is always cutting to pieces the veils of maya with the sword of knowledge. The inscrutable maya can never bring him under her control.

Ramakrishna, Calcutta, 10 December 1881, a few weeks after his first meeting with Narendra

The Panchavati at Dakshineswar where Ramakrishna, and later his disciples, practised many spiritual disciplines

Vivekananda narrated his days of joy at Dakshineswar:

Oh, what weird scenes things bring before me, the weirdest scenes of my whole life! Perfect silence, broken only by the cries of the jackals, in the darkness under the great tree at Dakshineswar. Night after night we sat there, the whole night through and he [Ramakrishna] talked to me, when I was a boy.

It is impossible to give others any idea of the ineffable joy we derived from the presence of the Master. It is really beyond our understanding how he could train us, without our knowing it, through fun and play, and thus mould our spiritual life. As the master wrestler proceeds with great caution and restraint with the beginner — now overpowering him in the struggle with great difficulty, as it were, and again allowing himself to be defeated to strengthen the pupil's self-confidence — in exactly the same manner did Sri Ramakrishna handle us. Realizing that the Atman [Self], the source of infinite strength, exists in every individual, pygmy though he might be, he was able to see the potential giant in all. He could clearly discern the latent spiritual power which would in the fullness of time manifest itself. Holding up that bright picture to view, he would speak highly of us and encourage us. Again he would warn us lest we should obstruct this future consummation by becoming entangled in worldly desires, and moreover he would keep us under control by carefully observing even the minute details of our life. All this was done silently and unobtrusively. That was the secret of his training of the disciples and of his moulding of their lives. . . .

Besides meditation and spiritual exercises, we used to spend a good deal of time there in sheer fun and merrymaking. Sri Ramakrishna also joined in with us, and by taking part, enhanced our innocent pleasure. We used to run and skip about, climb on the trees, swing from the creepers, and at times hold merry picnics. On the first day that we picnicked the Master noticed that I had cooked the food myself, and he partook of it. I knew that he could not take food unless it was cooked by brahmins, and therefore I had arranged for his meal at the Kali temple. But he said, "It won't be wrong for me to take food from such a pure soul as you." In spite of my repeated remonstrations, he enjoyed the food I had cooked that day.

Vivekananda, London, 1896

Knowing Naren's inherent nature, Sri Ramakrishna instructed him in monistic Vedanta, which teaches that the individual soul and Brahman are identical. One day Naren was telling Hazra about Vedantic nondualism and his unwillingness to accept it. "Can it be," he said, "that the waterpot is God, that the drinking vessel is God, that everything we see and all of us are God?" Naren laughed scornfully at the idea and Hazra joined in. While they were laughing, Ramakrishna came up to them. "What are you two talking about?" he asked Naren affectionately; then, without waiting for an answer, he touched Naren and went into samadhi. Naren related the effect of that touch:

At the marvellous touch of the Master, my mind underwent a complete revolution. I was aghast to realize that there really was nothing whatever in the entire universe but God. I remained silent, wondering how long this state of mind would continue. It didn't pass off all day. I got back home, and I felt just the same there; everything I saw was God. I sat down to eat, and I saw that everything — the plate, the food, my mother who was serving it, and I myself — everything was God and nothing else but God. I swallowed a couple of mouthfuls and then sat still without speaking. My mother asked me lovingly: "Why are you so quiet? Why don't you eat?" That brought me back to everyday consciousness, and I began eating again. But, from then on, I kept having the same experience, no matter what I was doing — eating, drinking, sitting, lying down, going to college, strolling along the street. It was a kind of intoxication; I can't describe it. If I were crossing a street and saw a carriage coming towards me I didn't have the urge, as I would ordinarily, to get out of its way for fear of being run over. For I said to myself: "I am that carriage. There's no difference between it and me." During that time, I had no sensation in my hands or my feet. When I ate food, I felt no satisfaction from it; it was as if someone else was eating. Sometimes I would lie down in the middle of a meal, and then get up again after a few minutes and go on eating. Thus it happened that on those days I would eat far more than usual, but this never upset me. My mother became alarmed; she thought I was suffering from some terrible disease. "He won't live long," she'd say.

When that first intoxication lost part of its power, I began to see the world as though it were in a dream. When I went for a walk around Cornwallis Square [now Azadhind Bag], I used to knock my head against the iron railings to find out if they were only dream railings or real ones. The loss of feeling in my hands and feet made me afraid that I was going to be paralyzed. When I did at last return to normal consciousness I felt convinced that the state I had been in was a revelation of nondualistic experience. So then I knew that what is written in the scriptures about this experience is all true.

My father's death in 1884 left my family in poverty. . . . One day the idea struck me that God listened to Sri Ramakrishna's prayers; so why should I not ask him to pray for me for the removal of my pecuniary needs — a favour the Master would never deny me? I hurried to Dakshineswar and insisted on his making the appeal on behalf of my starving family. He said: "My boy, I can't make such demands. But why don't you go and ask the Mother yourself? All your sufferings are due to your disregard of Her." I said, "I do not know the Mother; you please speak to Her on my behalf. You must." He replied tenderly: "My dear boy, I have done so again and again. But you do not accept Her, so She does not grant my prayer. All right, it is Tuesday — go to the Kali temple tonight, prostrate yourself before the Mother, and ask of Her any boon you like. It shall be granted. She is Knowledge Absolute, the Inscrutable Power of Brahman. By Her mere will She has given birth to this world. Everything is in Her power to give." I believed every word and eagerly waited for the night. About 9 o'clock the Master asked me to go to the temple. As I went, I was filled with a divine intoxication. My feet were unsteady. My heart was leaping in anticipation of the joy of beholding the living Goddess and hearing Her words. I was full of the idea. Reaching the temple, as I cast my eyes on the image, I actually found that the Divine Mother was living and conscious, the perennial fountain of Divine Love and Beauty. I was caught in a surging wave of devotion and love. In an ecstasy of joy I prostrated myself again and again before the Mother and prayed: "Mother, give me discrimination! Give me renunciation! Give me knowledge and devotion! Grant that I may have the uninterrupted vision of Thee!" A serene peace reigned in my soul. The world was forgotten. Only the Divine Mother shone within my heart.

As soon as I returned, the Master asked me if I had prayed to the Mother for the removal of my worldly needs. I was startled at this question and said: "No sir, I forgot all about it. But is there any remedy now?" "Go again," said he, "and tell Her about your needs." I again set out for the temple, but at the sight of the Mother again forgot my mission, bowed to Her repeatedly and prayed only for love and devotion. The Master asked me if I had done it the second time. I told him what had happened. He said: "How thought-

Mother Bhavatarini Kali at Dakshineswar

less! Couldn't you restrain yourself enough to say those few words? Well, try once more and make that prayer to Her. Quick!" I went for the third time, but on entering the temple a terrible shame overpowered me. I thought: "What a trifle I have come to pray to the Mother about! It is like asking a gracious king for a few vegetables! What a fool I am!" In shame and remorse I bowed to Her respectfully and said, "Mother, I want nothing but knowledge and devotion." Coming out of the temple I understood that all this was due to the Master's will. Otherwise how could I fail in my object no less than three times? I came to him and said: "Sir, it is you who have cast a charm over my mind and made me forgetful. Now please grant me the boon that my people at home may no longer suffer the pinch of poverty." He said: "Such a prayer never comes to my lips. I asked you to pray for yourself; but you couldn't do it. It seems that you are not destined to enjoy worldly happiness. Well, I can't help it." But I wouldn't let him go. I insisted on his granting that prayer. At last he said, "All right, your people at home will never be in want of plain food and clothing."

— *Vivekananda*

Cossipore garden house, where Ramakrishna lived during his last days (11 December 1885 to 16 August 1886)

Narendra: I was meditating here [Cossipore] last Saturday [2 January 1886], when suddenly I felt a peculiar sensation in my chest.

Mahendra: It was the awakening of the kundalini.

Narendra: Probably it was. I clearly perceived the Ida and Pingala nerves. I asked Hazra to feel my chest. Yesterday I saw him [meaning the Master] upstairs and told him about it. I said to him: "All the others had their realization [on the Kalpataru day, 1 January 1886]; please give me something. All have succeeded; shall I alone remain unsatisfied?" He said, "Why don't you settle your family affairs and then come to me? You will get everything. What do you want?" I replied, "It is my desire to remain absorbed in samadhi continually for three or four days, only once in a while coming down to the sense plane to eat a little food." Thereupon he said, "You are a small-minded person. There is a state higher even than that. 'All that exists art Thou': it is you who sing that song. Settle your family affairs and then come to me. You will attain a state higher than samadhi."

I went home this morning. My people scolded me, saying: "Why do you wander about like a vagabond? Your Law examination is near at hand and you are not paying any attention to your studies. You wander about aimlessly." I went to my study at my grandmother's. As I tried to read I was seized with a great fear, as if studying were a terrible thing. My heart struggled within me. I burst into tears. I never wept so bitterly in my life. I left my books and ran away. I ran past a haystack and got hay all over me. I kept on running along the road here [Cossipore].

The description of Narendra's nirvikalpa samadhi:

One evening he was absorbed in his usual meditation when he suddenly felt as if a lamp were burning at the back of his head. The light glowed more and more intensely and finally burst. Narendra was overwhelmed by that light and fell unconscious. After some time, as he began to regain his normal mood, he could feel only his head and not the rest of his body.

In an agitated voice he said to Gopal, a brother disciple who was meditating in the same room, "Where is my body?"

Gopal answered: "Why, Naren, it is there. Don't you feel it?"

Gopal was afraid that Narendra was dying, and ran to Sri Ramakrishna's room. He found the Master in a calm but serious mood, evidently aware of what had happened in the room downstairs. After listening to Gopal the Master said, "Let him stay in that state for a while; he has pestered me long enough for it."

For a long time Narendra remained unconscious, and when he regained his normal state of mind he was bathed in an ineffable peace. As he entered Sri Ramakrishna's room the latter said: "Now the Mother has shown you everything. But this realization, like the jewel locked in a box, will be hidden away from you and kept in my custody. I will keep the key with me. Only after you have fulfilled your mission on this earth will the box be unlocked, and you will know everything as you have known it now."

Narendra's own words:

One day in the Cossipore garden, I expressed my prayer [for nirvikalpa samadhi] to Sri Ramakrishna with great earnestness. Then in the evening, at the hour of meditation, I lost consciousness of the body and felt that it was absolutely nonexistent. I felt that the sun, moon, space, time, ether, and all had been reduced to a homogeneous mass and then melted far away into the unknown. Body-consciousness almost vanished, and I nearly merged in the Supreme. But I had just a trace of the feeling of ego so I could again return to the world of relativity from samadhi. In this state of samadhi all difference between "I" and "Brahman" goes away, everything is reduced to unity, like the water of the Infinite Ocean — water everywhere, nothing else exists. Language and thought, all fail there. Then only is the state "beyond mind and speech" realized in its actuality. Otherwise, as long as the religious aspirant thinks or says, "I am Brahman" — "I" and "Brahman," these two entities persist — there is the involved semblance of duality. After that experience, even after trying repeatedly, I failed to bring back the state of samadhi. On informing Sri Ramakrishna about it, he said: "If you remain day and night in that state, the work of the Divine Mother will not be accomplished. Therefore you won't be able to induce that state again. When your work is finished, it will come again."

Cossipore, 1886

Cossipore garden house, 16 August 1886. (This group picture was taken with Sri Ramakrishna's dead body, which has been masked in keeping with the custom of the Ramakrishna Order.) *(Narendra ↑)*

Vivekananda to a disciple:

Two or three days before Sri Ramakrishna's passing away, She whom he used to call "Kali" entered this body. It is She who takes me here and there and makes me work, without letting me remain quiet or allowing me to look to my personal comforts.

Before his leaving the body, he called me to his side one day, and asking me to sit before him, looked steadily at me and went into samadhi. Then I felt that a subtle force like an electric shock was entering my body! In a little while I also lost outward consciousness and sat motionless. How long I stayed in that condition I do not remember. When consciousness returned I found Sri Ramakrishna shedding tears. On questioning him, he answered me affectionately: "Today, giving you my all, I have become a beggar. With this power you are to do much work for the good of the world before you return." I feel that that power is constantly directing me to this or that work. This body has not been made for remaining idle.

Cossipore garden house, 16 August 1886

1 Atul
2 Amrita
3 Vaikuntha Nath Sannyal
4 Bhavanath Chatterjee
5 Baburam *(Swami Premananda)*
6 Narendra *(Swami Vivekananda)*
7 Ram Chandra Datta
8 Gopal Ghosh *(Swami Advaitananda)*
9 Sharat *(Swami Saradananda)*
10 Balaram Bose
11 Latu *(Swami Adbhutananda)*
12 Shashi *(Swami Ramakrishnananda)*
13 Rakhal *(Swami Brahmananda)*
14 Nityagopal
15 Jogindra *(Swami Yogananda)*
16 Devendra Nath Mazumdar
17 Tarak *(Swami Shivananda)*
18 Young Gopal
19 Nitya Niranjan *(Swami Niranjanananda)*
20 Narayan
21 Manilal Mallick
22 Fakir
23 Surendra
24 Bhupati
25 Harish
26 Girindra
27 Binod
28 M. *(Mahendra Nath Gupta)*
29 Kali *(Swami Abhedananda)*
30 Navagopal Ghosh
31 Gangadhar *(Swami Akhandananda)*
32 Mahimacharan
33 Manomohan Mitra

Disciple: Did Sri Ramakrishna, out of his own lips, ever say that he was God, the all-perfect Brahman?

Vivekananda: Yes, he did so many times. And he said this to all of us. One day while he was staying at the Cossipore garden, his body in imminent danger of falling off forever, by the side of his bed I was saying in my mind: "Well, now if you can declare that you are God, then only will I believe you are really God Himself." It was only two days before he passed away. Immediately, he looked up towards me all on a sudden and said: "He who was Rama, He who was Krishna, verily is He now Ramakrishna in this body. And that not merely from the standpoint of your Vedanta [which substantiates that each soul is potentially divine]!" At this I was struck dumb. ❧

III

Years of Travel as a Wandering Monk

After Ramakrishna's passing away on 16 August 1886, Vivekananda and some of the other disciples established the first Ramakrishna Math (monastery) at Baranagore, and then in the early part of 1887 they took formal monastic vows. They studied the scriptures, practised severe austerity and meditation, and thus prepared themselves to be world teachers.

There is a saying, "The monk is pure who goes and the river is pure which flows." In 1888 Vivekananda left the monastery to live as a penniless, wandering monk. He carried a staff, a waterpot, and his two favourite books — the *Bhagavad Gita* and *The Imitation of Christ*.

He first went to Varanasi, the City of Light and centre of ancient Indian culture. During his journey he met many holy people and scholars. He knew the mission of his life and felt a tremendous power inside himself. He left Varanasi with these prophetic words: "When I return here the next time, I shall burst upon society like a bombshell, and it will follow me like a dog." He then visited the holy places of northern India and the Himalayas.

During his itinerant days, he had various spiritual experiences. Once, in a vision, he saw an old man standing on the bank of the Indus river chanting Vedic hymns. He distinctly heard the invocation of the Gayatri mantra from the Rig Veda. The swami believed that through this vision he had rediscovered the musical cadences of the early Aryans. He experienced the presence of the Cosmic God in all beings.

He travelled over almost all of India, mostly on foot, visiting places of pilgrimage. He was thus able to have firsthand experience of the lives of the people. Seeing the pitiable living conditions of the masses, he was at times moved to tears. Only one who has suffered can understand the sufferings of others. Once he remarked, with his usual vigour, that a God who could not in this life give a crust of bread was not to be trusted in the next for the kingdom of heaven. He observed that religion was not the crying need of India, and recalled Sri Ramakrishna's pithy saying, "Religion is not for an empty stomach." He tried to draw the attention of the local rulers to the deplorable conditions of the masses, but did not get much response. Later, he expressed his feelings: "May I be born again and again, and suffer thousands of miseries so that I may worship the only God that exists, the only God I believe in, the sum total of all souls — and above all, my God the wicked, my God the miserable, my God the poor of all races, of all species, is the special object of my worship."

While travelling in India, Vivekananda heard about the Parliament of Religions that was to be held at Chicago in September 1893. Some Indian rulers and influential people requested that he attend and represent Hinduism, but he refused. Later, when in a vision he heard the command of Sri Ramakrishna, he agreed to go.

Vivekananda left for America on 31 May 1893. Before his departure, he said to Turiyananda: "Brother Hari, I am going to America. Whatever you hear of as happening there [meaning preparations for the Parliament of Religions], is all for this [striking his own chest]. For this [me] alone everything is being arranged."

Painting of Ramakrishna by Frank Dvorak, an Austrian artist

One day, when Surendra Nath Mitra, a devotee of the Master who used to bear a part of the expenses at the Cossipore garden house, returned home from his office and sat for meditation in his shrine, Sri Ramakrishna appeared before him and said: "Oh! What are you doing? My children are wandering in the streets. Look at their sad plight! Make some arrangement for them without delay." Hearing this command of the Master, Surendra hastened to Narendra's home, which was nearby, and with tearful eyes told him what had happened. He said: "Brother, where will you go? Let us rent a house. You will live there and make it our Master's shrine; and we householders shall go there from time to time to share your bliss and pacify our hearts. . . . I used to spend a sum of money for the Master at Cossipore. I shall gladly give it now for your expenses." Narendra was overwhelmed with emotion on hearing this.

After an extensive search a house was found at Baranagore, midway between Dakshineswar and Calcutta. It was a dreary, deserted place, sadly in need of repairs, very old, and with the reputation of being haunted. It had two storeys, the lower one the resort of snakes and lizards. The gateway had long since tumbled down. The veranda which ran along the front of the upper storey showed signs of decay. The main room where the monks were to live was in a most dilapidated state; indeed, nobody else would have lived there. . . .

It was chosen because of its cheapness and its nearness to the holy Ganges and the Cossipore burning-ghat where the body of the Master had been cremated. The monks were pleased with it, for it provided not only a retreat from the turmoil of city life, but also a place of solitude where their meditation would have few or no interruptions. The house was taken at a monthly rent of eleven rupees inclusive of tax.

Surendra Nath Mitra (1850-1890)

Ramakrishna Monastery at Baranagore

The members of the Math [monastery] called themselves the "danas" and the "daityas," which mean the "ghosts" and the "demons," the companions of Shiva. They took these names because of their utter indifference to worldly pleasures and relationships.

The southernmost room of the second floor was used for meditation, contemplation, and study, and was known as Kali Tapasvi's room, since Kali used to shut himself in there most of the day. North of this room was the worship room, and north of that, again, was the room where the offerings for the worship were prepared. From this room the devotees used to watch the evening worship. North of the "offering room" was the room of the "danas," a very long hall where the members of the Math used to assemble. Here the householder devotees and visitors were received. North of this hall was a small room where the devotees took their meals. East of the worship room and of Kali Tapasvi's room ran a long veranda, at the southwest corner of which was the library of a society of Baranagore. Between Kali Tapasvi's room and this library was a staircase; and north of the dining room was another staircase, leading to the roof.

Narendra and the other members of the Math often spent their evenings on this roof. There they devoted a great deal of time to discussion of the teachings of Sri Ramakrishna, Sankaracharya, Ramanuja, and Jesus Christ, and of Hindu philosophy, European philosophy, the Vedas, the Puranas, and the Tantras.

Vivekananda

Brahmananda

Yogananda

Niranjanananda

Adbhutananda

Premananda

Shivananda

Turiyananda

Saradananda

Ramakrishnananda

Abhedananda

Akhandananda

Advaitananda

Trigunatitananda

Subodhananda

Vijnanananda

he monastic names of Ramakrishna's intimate disciples who renounced the world soon after his death were as follows:

Narendra. . . . . *Swami Vivekananda*
Rakhal. . . . . *Swami Brahmananda*
Jogin . . . . *Swami Yogananda*
Niranjan . . . . *Swami Niranjanananda*
Latu . . . . *Swami Adbhutananda*
Baburam . . . . *Swami Premananda*
Tarak . . . . *Swami Shivananda*
Hari . . . . *Swami Turiyananda*
Sharat . . . . *Swami Saradananda*
Shashi . . . . *Swami Ramakrishnananda*
Kali . . . . *Swami Abhedananda*
Gangadhar . . . . *Swami Akhandananda*
Gopal (elder). . . . . *Swami Advaitananda*
Sarada Prasanna . . . . . *Swami Trigunatitananda*
Subodh . . . . *Swami Subodhananda*
Hariprasanna . . . . *Swami Vijnanananda*

Baranagore Math, 1887
Standing, left to right: *Swamis Shivananda, Ramakrishnananda, and Vivekananda, the monastery cook, Devendra Mazumdar, Mahendra Nath Gupta (M.), Swami Trigunatitananda, Mustaphi (maternal uncle of Devendra Mazumdar).* Sitting, left to right: *Swamis Niranjanananda and Saradananda, Hutko Gopal, Swami Abhedananda.*

After the passing away of Sri Ramakrishna we underwent a lot of religious practice at the Baranagore Math. We used to get up at 3 a.m. and after washing our faces, etc. — some after a bath, and others without it — we would sit in the worship-room and become absorbed in japa and meditation. What a strong spirit of dispassion we had in those days! We had no thought even as to whether the world existed or not. Ramakrishnananda busied himself day and night with the duties pertaining to Sri Ramakrishna's worship and service, and occupied the same position in the Math as the mistress of the house does in a family. It was he who would procure, mostly by begging, the requisite articles for Sri Ramakrishna's worship and our subsistence. There have been days when the japa and meditation continued from morning till four or five in the afternoon. Ramakrishnananda waited and waited with our meals ready, till at last he would come and snatch us from our meditation by sheer force. Oh, what a wonderful constancy of devotion we have noticed in him! . . .

There have been days when the Math was without a grain of food. If some rice was collected by begging, there was no salt to take it with! On some days there would be only rice and salt, but nobody cared about that in the least. We were then being carried away by a tidal wave of spiritual practice. Boiled Bimba leaves, rice, and salt — this was the menu for a month at a stretch. Oh, those wonderful days!

— *Vivekananda*

One morning, after visiting the temple of Mother Durga [in Varanasi], Vivekananda was passing through a place where there were a large tank of water on one side and a high wall on the other. Here he was surrounded by a troop of large monkeys. They were not willing to allow him to pass along that way. They howled and shrieked and clutched at his feet as he strode. As they pressed closer, he began to run; but the faster he ran, the faster came the monkeys, and they began to bite at him. When it seemed impossible for him to escape, he heard an old sannyasin calling out to him: "Face the brutes." The words brought him to his senses. He turned and boldly faced the irate monkeys. As soon as he did that, they fell back and fled. With reverence and gratitude he gave the traditional greeting to the sannyasin, who smilingly responded with the same, and walked away. In a New York lecture years later, the swami referred to this incident and pointed to its moral: "That is a lesson for all life — face the terrible, face it boldly. Like the monkeys, the hardships of life fall back when we cease to flee before them. If we are ever to gain freedom, it must be by conquering nature, never by running away. Cowards never win victories. We have to fight fear and troubles and ignorance if we expect them to flee before us."

Durga Temple at Varanasi

Varanasi bathing ghat

ASSOCIATING WITH PAVHARI BABA, I got to like him very much; and he also came to love me deeply. One day I reflected that I had not learnt any art for making this weak body strong, even though I had lived with Sri Ramakrishna for so many years. I had heard that Pavhari Baba knew the science of hatha yoga; so I thought that I would learn the practices of hatha yoga from him, and through them strengthen the body. You know, I have a dogged resolution, and whatever I set my heart on, I always carry out. On the eve of the

Pavhari Baba's Ashrama, Gazipur (near Varanasi)

day on which I was to take initiation, I was lying on a cot thinking; and just then I saw the form of Sri Ramakrishna standing on my right, looking steadfastly at me, as if very much grieved. I had dedicated myself to him, and at the thought that I was taking another guru I felt much ashamed and kept looking at him. Thus perhaps two or three hours passed, but no words escaped my mouth: then he disappeared all on a sudden. Seeing Sri Ramakrishna that night my mind became upset, so I postponed the idea of initiation from Pavhari Baba for the day. After a day or two, again the idea of initiation from Pavhari Baba arose in the mind — and again at night Sri Ramakrishna appeared, as on the previous occasion. So when, for twenty-one nights in succession, I had the vision of Sri Ramakrishna, I gave up the idea of initiation altogether, thinking that since every time I resolved on it, I was having such a vision, no good, but only harm, would come of it.

— *Vivekananda*

The cave where Pavhari Baba used to meditate.

Taj Mahal at Agra

The artistry and workmanship of Indian artisans astounded him [Vivekananda]; the beauty of the Taj Mahal overpowered him. He visited it many times, seeing it from different angles, in every light, and above all in the perspective of his love for India. He used to say, "Every square inch of this wondrous edifice is worth a whole day's patient observation, and it requires at least six months to make a real study of it!" The magnificent fort of Agra stimulated his historical imagination. Walking through the streets of the city with its palaces and tombs, he saw the whole Mogul era unfold before him.

While going round the Govardhan Hill [Vrindaban], the swami vowed that he would not beg his food from anyone, that he would eat only what was offered to him without asking. During the first day he became exceedingly hungry at noon. To add to his discomfort, heavy rain began to fall. He grew faint with hunger and with much walking, but still went on and on, without asking for food. Suddenly he heard someone calling him from behind, but he did not answer. Nearer and nearer came the voice, that of a devotee, calling out that he had brought food for him. The swami began to run as fast as he could, to test this apparent act of Providence. The man, running after him for nearly a mile, overtook him and insisted

Kaliyadaman Ghat, Vrindaban

that he accept the food. The swami accepted it, saying nothing. Shortly after, the man disappeared among the trees. Ecstatic with devotion at this miraculous act of the Lord, and with tears streaming from his eyes, the swami cried out, "Glory to Sri Radha! Glory to Sri Krishna!" In the wilderness the Lord had taken care of his devotee.

On his way to Hardwar, Vivekananda stopped at the Hathras railroad station. Sharat Chandra Gupta, the assistant stationmaster, met Swamiji and became his disciple. He resigned from the job and followed his guru.

Hathras station, North India

"Once in our wanderings in the outlying districts of the Himalayas," said Sharat much later, "I fainted with hunger and thirst. The swami carried me and thus undoubtedly saved me from certain death. On another occasion, like a syce he led the horse, which someone had kindly lent us for the journey, across a mountain river which was very dangerous to ford because of its swiftness and slippery bottom. He risked his life several times for my sake. How can I describe him, friends, except by the word Love, Love, Love! When I was too ill to do anything but stagger along, he carried my personal belongings including my shoes." It is not strange then, that in later life feeling forlorn once and asking the swami whether he was going to give him [Sharat] up, the swami should answer with a sweet severity, "Fool, do you not remember that I have carried even your shoes!"

Swami Sadananda (Sharat Chandra Gupta), Vivekananda's first disciple.

Still another time, as the swami and his disciple were moving through the jungle, they came across some bleached human bones, with pieces of rotting ochre cloth lying here and there. "See," said the swami, "here a tiger has devoured a sannyasin! Are you afraid?" The disciple promptly replied, "Not with you, Swamiji!" Even in those early days when he was an unknown monk, the force of the swami's character and his power to inspire others could be plainly seen.

Hardwar, the foothill of the Himalayas

Rishikesh, a place for hermits

As soon as you say, "I am bound," "I am weak," "I am helpless," woe unto you; you rivet one more chain upon yourself. Do not say it, do not think it. I have heard of a man who lived in a forest and used to repeat day and night, "Shivoham" — I am the Blessed One — and one day a tiger fell upon him and dragged him away to kill him; people on the other side of the river saw it, and heard the voice so long as voice remained in him, saying, "Shivoham" — even in the very jaws of the tiger. There have been many such men. There have been cases of men who, while being cut to pieces, have blessed their enemies. "I am He, I am He; and so art thou. I am pure and perfect, and so are all my enemies. You are He, and so am I."

— *Vivekananda*

"I SAW MANY GREAT MEN IN RISHIKESH," said the swami in later life: "One that I remember was a man who seemed to be mad. He was coming nude down the street, with boys pursuing him and throwing stones at him. The whole man was bubbling over with laughter, while blood was streaming down his face and neck. I took him and bathed his wound, putting ashes (made by burning a piece of cotton cloth) on it to stop the bleeding. And all the time, with peals of laughter, he told me of the fun the boys and he had been having, throwing the stones. 'So the Father plays,' he said. Many of these holy men hide in order to guard themselves against intrusion. People are a trouble to them. One had human bones strewn about his cave and gave it out that he lived on corpses. Another threw stones, and so on." The swami continued, "The sannyasin needs no longer to worship or to go on pilgrimage or perform austerities. What, then, is the motive of all this going from pilgrimage to pilgrimage, shrine to shrine, and austerity to austerity? He is acquiring merit, and giving it to the world!"

Peepul tree at Kakrighat, on the way to Almora

At Kakrighat Vivekananda said to Akhandananda: "Oh, Gangadhar! I have just passed through one of the greatest moments of my life. Here under this peepul tree one of the greatest problems of my life has been solved. I have found the oneness of the macrocosm with the microcosm. In this microcosm of the body everything that is there [in the macrocosm], exists. I have seen the whole universe within an atom." For that whole day the swami was in a high state of mind and discussed his realization with his companion. The fragments he wrote in Bengali in his notebook then, read:

"In the beginning was the Word, etc.

"The microcosm and the macrocosm are built on the same plan. Just as the individual soul is encased in the living body, so is the universal Soul in the Living Prakriti [Nature] — the objective universe. Shivā [i.e. Kali] is embracing Shiva: this is not a fancy. This covering of the one [Soul] by the other [Nature] is analogous to the relation between an idea and the word expressing it: they are one and the same; and it is only by a mental abstraction that one can distinguish them. Thought is impossible without words. Therefore, in the beginning was the Word, etc.

"This dual aspect of the Universal Soul is eternal. So what we perceive or feel is this combination of the Eternally Formed and the Eternally Formless."

This realization of his seems to be reflected in the lectures he later gave in the West under the title, "Cosmos — the Macrocosm and the Microcosm."

Vivekananda as an itinerant monk, Madras, 1893

(probably) Jaipur, 1891

Many times I have been in the jaws of death, starving, footsore, and weary; for days and days I had had no food, and often could walk no farther; I would sink down under a tree, and life would seem to be ebbing away. I could not speak, I could scarcely think, but at last the mind reverted to the idea: "I have no fear nor death; never was I born, never did I die; I never hunger or thirst. I am It! I am It! The whole of nature cannot crush me; it is my servant. Assert thy strength, thou Lord of lords and God of gods! Regain thy lost empire! Arise and walk and stop not!" And I would rise up, reinvigorated; and here I am today, living! Thus, whenever darkness comes, assert the reality, and everything adverse must vanish. For, after all, it is but a dream. Mountain-high though the difficulties appear, terrible and gloomy though all things seem, they are but maya. Fear not, and it is banished. Crush it, and it vanishes. Stamp upon it and it dies. Be not afraid. Think not how many times you fail. Never mind — time is infinite. Go forward. Assert yourself again and again, and light must come.

— *Vivekananda*

The Himalayas

Maharaja Mangal Singh of Alwar said to Vivekananda: "Well, Swamiji Maharaj, I have no faith in idol-worship. What is going to be my fate?" He smiled as he spoke. The swami seemed slightly annoyed and exclaimed, "Surely you are joking." "No, Swamiji, not at all. You see, I really cannot worship wood, earth, stone or metal, like other people. Does this mean that I shall fare worse in the life hereafter?" The swami answered, "Well, I suppose every man should follow the religious ideal according to his own faith." The devotees of the swami were perplexed at this reply, for they knew that the swami sanctioned image-worship. But the swami had not finished; his eyes lighted on a picture of the Maharaja which was hanging on the wall. At his request it was passed to him. Holding it in his hand he asked, "Whose picture is this?" The Dewan [minister] answered, "It is the likeness of our Maharaja." A moment later they trembled with fear when they heard the swami commanding the Dewan: "Spit on it."

The Dewan cried out: "What, Swamiji! What are you asking me to do? This is the likeness of our Maharaja! How can I do such a thing?" "Be it so," said the swami, "but the Maharaja is not bodily present in this photograph. This is only a piece of paper. It does not contain his bones and flesh and blood. It does not speak or behave or move in any way as the Maharaja does; yet all of you refuse to spit on it, because you see in this photo the shadow of the Maharaja. Indeed, in spitting on the photo, you feel that you insult your master, the Prince himself."

Turning to the Maharaja he continued, "See, Your Highness; though this is not you in one sense, in another sense it is you. That was why your devoted servants were so perplexed when I asked them to spit on it. It is a shadow of you; it brings you into their minds. One glance at it makes them see you in it; therefore they look at it with as much respect as they would have in looking at your own person. Thus it also is with the devotees who worship stone and metal images of gods and goddesses. It is because an image brings to their minds their Ishta, or some special form and attributes of the Divinity, and helps them to concentrate, that the devotees worship God in an image. They do not worship the stone or the metal as such."

Mangal Singh, who had been listening attentively all this time, said, with folded hands: "Swamiji, I must admit that, looking at image-worship in the light you have thrown on it, I have never yet met anyone who worshipped stone, or wood, or metal. Before this I did not understand its meaning. You have opened my eyes."

(probably) Jaipur, 1891

In Khetri an incident occurred that the swami remembered all his life. He was invited by the Maharaja to a musical entertainment in which a nautch-girl was to sing, and he refused to come, since he was a monk and not permitted to enjoy secular pleasures. The singer was hurt and sang in a strain of lamentation. Her words reached the swami's ears:

Look not, O Lord, upon my sins!
Is not Same-sightedness Thy name?
One piece of iron is used
Inside the holy shrine,
Another for the knife
Held in the butcher's hand;
Yet both of these are turned to gold
When touched by the philosophers' stone.
Sacred the Jumna's water,
Foul the water in the ditch;
Yet both alike are sanctified
Once they have joined the Ganges' stream.
So, Lord, look not upon my sins!
Is not Same-sightedness Thy name?

Maharaja Ajit Singh of Khetri

Belgaum, October 1892

The swami was deeply moved. This girl, whom society condemned as impure, had taught him a great lesson: Brahman, the Ever Pure, Ever Free, and Ever Illumined, is the essence of all beings. Before God there is no distinction of good and evil, pure and impure. Such pairs of opposites become manifest only when the light of Brahman is obscured by maya. A sannyasin ought to look at all things from the standpoint of Brahman. He should not condemn anything, even a so-called impure person.

The swami then joined the party and with tears in his eyes said to the girl: "Mother, I am guilty. I was about to show you disrespect by refusing to come to this room. But your song awakened my consciousness."

My noble Prince [the Maharaja of Mysore], this life is short, the vanities of the world are transient, but they alone live who live for others, the rest are more dead than alive. One such high, noble-minded and royal son of India as your Highness can do much towards raising India on her feet again and thus leave a name to posterity which shall be worshipped.

— *Vivekananda*

Of the Raja of Ramnad, the swami said:

India owes much to this good man, for it was he who conceived the idea of my going to Chicago, and it was he who put the idea into my head and persistently urged me to accomplish it.

Sri Chamaraja Wadiyar, Maharaja of Mysore

Bhaskara Setupati, Raja of Ramnad

Vivekananda Rock (centre), Kanya Kumari, where he meditated and spent three nights during Christmas week in 1892. A memorial temple of Vivekananda now adorns the rock.

At Cape Comorin [24-26 December 1892], sitting in Mother Kumari's temple, sitting on the last bit of Indian rock, I hit upon a plan: We are so many sannyasins, wandering about and teaching the people metaphysics — it is all madness. Did not our gurudeva use to say, "An empty stomach is no good for religion?" That these poor people are leading the life of brutes is simply due to ignorance. We have for all ages been sucking their blood and trampling them underfoot.

— *Vivekananda*

After worshipping the Virgin Mother, he came out from the temple and saw a beautiful rock in the ocean, a couple of furlongs from the mainland. As he had no money to pay to the ferryman, he swam through the shark-infested water and reached there for meditation. His great journey from the Himalayas to the Indian Ocean was completed. He stayed on that isolated islet for three days during Christmas week in 1892, and pondered his mission. There flashed before his mind the new continent of America, a land of optimism, great wealth, and unstinted generosity. He decided to give the receptive Americans the ancient wisdom of India and bring back to his motherland, in exchange, the knowledge of science and technology. If he succeeded in his mission to America, he would not only enhance India's prestige in the West, but create a new confidence among his own people. He recalled the earnest requests of his friends to represent India at the forthcoming Parliament of Religions in Chicago.

Mother Kumari at Kanya Kumari Temple

It was at Pondicherry [near Madras] that the swami had a heated discussion with a bigoted pandit on topics relating to Hinduism and its reform. The pandit, being of the old school, opposed the swami at every turn. He was more bellicose than learned, and he became fierce in his denunciation of the swami's progressive ideas. The conversation turned to the question of going overseas. The swami told the pandit that the time had come for Hinduism to take a look at itself; for it to contrast its glories, culture and worth with those of Western civilization; and for it to adjust itself to modern needs and problems, without sacrificing essentials. The pandit met these remarks with violent denunciation, saying that Hinduism was not in need of any reform, that Westerners were all Mlechchhas [non-Hindus], and that contact with the West would pervert the Hindu people. . . . In the end the pandit was able to appreciate the force of the swami's reasoning, though he still maintained that the Kalapani, or "black water" of the ocean, was the great dividing-line between the land of the Hindus and the lands of the Mlechchhas, and was never to be crossed.

Trivandrum, December 1892

Alasinga Perumal

During March and April [1893] the swami's disciples in Madras took definite steps to raise subscriptions for his passage to America. Some even went to Mysore, Ramnad and Hyderabad for the purpose. They visited those whom the swami had made his disciples, or who were his avowed admirers. Those who had organized themselves into a subscription committee, had, as their leader, Alasinga Perumal, a devoted follower of the swami. He did not hesitate to beg from door to door. It was he and the young men under him who collected the major portion of the funds. They went for the most part to the middle classes, for the swami had told them: "If it is the Mother's will that I go, then let me receive the money from the people! Because it is for the people of India that I am going to the West — for the people and the poor!"

Holy Mother (Sarada Devi, the wife of Ramakrishna)

The Bay of Bengal, Madras

In Madras the swami one day had a symbolic dream, in which he saw Sri Ramakrishna walking into the water of the ocean and beckoning him to follow. He also heard the authoritative word "Go!"

Although Swamiji was now certain of his journey, he still felt it necessary to have Holy Mother's permission and blessings. He wrote to Swami Saradananda: "I have had a vision in which the Master is telling me to go to the West. My mind is quite disturbed. Please tell Holy Mother everything and let me know her opinion." Swami Saradananda went to Holy Mother and read Swamiji's letter to her. Holy Mother did not give her opinion immediately, but asked Saradananda to wait. After a couple of days, she told Saradananda, "Please write to Naren that he should go to the West." Before giving her permission, Holy Mother had had a dream. She saw the Master walking over the ocean waves and asking Narendra to follow him. Swamiji was overjoyed when he received Holy Mother's approval and blessings.

Madras, 1893

The Empress of India, which Vivekananda took from Yokohama to Vancouver, Canada

In May 1893, on his way to Bombay the swami stopped at the Abu Road station and met Brahmananda and Turiyananda. He told them about his going to America. The two brother disciples were greatly excited. He explained to them the reason for his going; it was India's suffering. "I travelled," he said, "all over India. But alas, it was agony to me, my brothers, to see with my own eyes the terrible poverty of the masses, and I could not restrain my tears! It is now my firm conviction that to preach religion amongst them, without first trying to remove their poverty and suffering, is futile. It is for this reason — to find means for the salvation of the poor of India — that I am going to America."

Addressing Turiyananda, he said, "Brother, I cannot understand your so-called religion." His face was red with his rising blood. Shaking with emotion, he placed his hand on his heart, and said: "But my heart has grown much, much larger, and I have learned to feel. Believe me, I feel it very sadly." He was choked, and then fell silent. Tears rolled down his cheeks.

Many years later Turiyananda said, while describing the incident: "You can imagine what went through my mind when I heard these pathetic words and saw the majestic sadness of Swamiji. 'Were not these,' I thought, 'the very words and feelings of Buddha?' " ❧

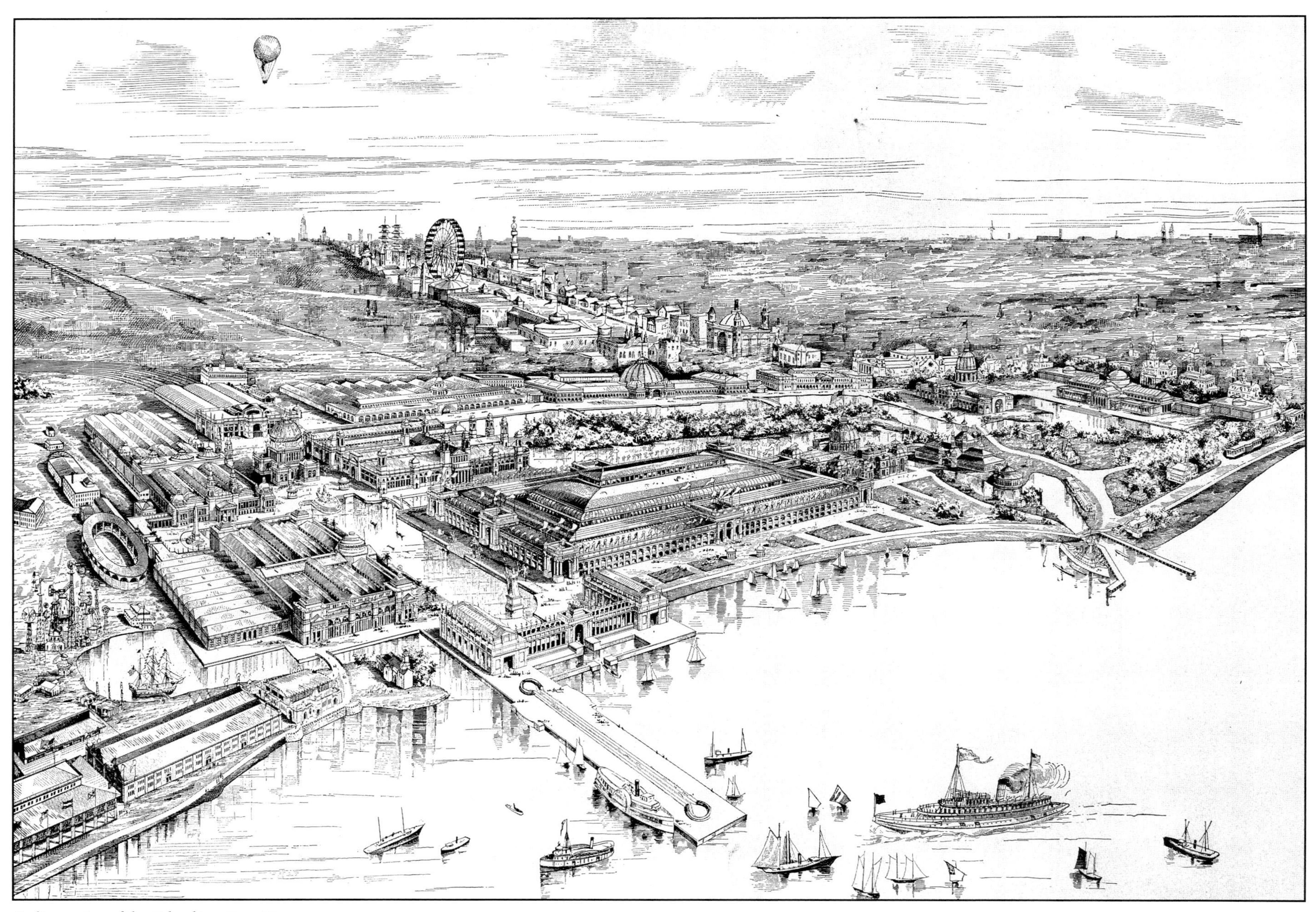

Bird's eye view of the Columbian Exposition

IV

The Columbian Exposition at Chicago in 1893

Vivekananda reached Chicago on 30 July 1893 via Colombo, Penang, Singapore, Hong Kong, Canton, Nagasaki, Kobe, Osaka, Kyoto, Tokyo, Yokohama, Vancouver, and Winnipeg. Soon after his arrival in Chicago, he went to the information bureau of the Columbian Exposition and heard some heartrending news: the forthcoming Parliament of Religions would not open before the second week of September; no one without credentials from a bona fide organization would be accepted as a delegate; the date to be registered as a delegate had passed. Moreover, he knew no one in Chicago and he did not have sufficient money to pay the exorbitant hotel charges.

Nevertheless, he stayed in Chicago for nearly two weeks and attended the World's Fair, which had been arranged in connection with the four-hundred-year anniversary of Columbus's discovery of America. "The primary purpose of the World's Columbian Exposition of 1893," writes Marie Louise Burke, "was to bring together the fruits of Man's material progress. Everything imaginable was on exhibit — not only the achievements of Western civilization, but the better to show these off, life-size models of the more backward cultures of the world."

Dr. Alfred Momerie, an English scholar, said: "I have seen all the great exhibitions of Europe during the last fifteen years, and I can safely say that the World's Columbian Exposition is greater than all of them put together, and the Parliament of Religions is, in my opinion, greater than the Exposition."

God acts in mysterious ways. Someone suggested that Vivekananda go to Boston, where living expenses would be much cheaper. Previously while travelling from Vancouver to Chicago, he had met Katherine Sanborn of Boston on the train. She had invited him to be her guest. So he left for Boston, and became her guest. She introduced Vivekananda to John Wright, a professor of Greek at Harvard University. Professor Wright wrote some letters of introduction for Vivekananda to take to friends who were connected with the Parliament, and then sent him back to Chicago.

Vivekananda arrived late one evening; unfortunately, he had lost the address of the committee in charge of the delegates. He did not know where to turn for help, and nobody came forward to assist this strange looking foreigner. He passed that night without food in an empty wagon at the Chicago train station. The next morning, by divine providence, he met Mrs. George W. Hale. She took him into her home and later introduced him to her personal friend, Dr. J. H. Barrows, the President of the Parliament. Thus the swami was accepted as a representative of Hinduism and was lodged with the other delegates.

In spite of opposition from various Christian denominations, including the Archbishop of Canterbury, the advisory committee had adopted ten objectives for the Parliament of Religions. The important ones were: (1) To bring together in conference, for the first time in history, the leading representatives of the great historic religions of the world. (2) To show to humanity, in the most impressive way, what and how many important truths the various religions hold and teach in common. (3) To inquire what light each religion has afforded, or may afford, to the other religions of the world. (4) To discover, from competent men, what light religion has to throw on the great problems of the present age. (5) To bring the nations of the earth into a more friendly fellowship, in the hope of securing permanent international peace.

Poster of the Parliament of Religions, Chicago World's fair, 1893

Basin and Court of Honour at the World's Fair seen from behind the statue of the Republic. Buildings from left to right: Agriculture, Machinery, Administration, Electricity, and Manufactures.

Any tour of the World's Columbian Exposition should begin in the southern part of the grounds with the Court of Honour, the real White City. The Court consisted of a number of the noblest buildings, the porticos and arcades of which — though remaining inside the building lines — formed a continuous stoa around a Basin 350 feet wide and 1,100 feet long.

On the day following his arrival in Chicago, Vivekananda set out to visit the World's Fair. He was struck with amazement at the wonders he saw. Here all the latest products of the inventive and artistic minds of the entire world had been brought to a focus, as it were, for examination and admiration. He visited the various exposition palaces, marvelling at the array of machinery, at the arts and products of many lands, and, above all, at the energy and practical acumen of the human mind as manifested by the exhibits. Yet, among the streams of visitors to the Fair, he at first felt desperately lonely; for in all that vast crowd, indeed in the whole continent of North America, he had not one friend. Soon, however, people now and then approached the swami, desiring to know who he was. He continued to frequent the Fair, eager to absorb all that was of value. He was fascinated by the splendour and perfect organization of it all.

Above: The Chicago day crowd in the Grand Plaza in front of Administration and on the bridge between Machinery and Agriculture. Below: The Columbian Fountain, from the south. In the background: left, main entrance to Electricity; right, Manufactures.

YOU HAVE SEEN THE BIG FERRIS WHEEL IN CHICAGO. The wheel revolves, and the little rooms in the wheel are regularly coming one after another; one set of persons gets into these, and after they have gone round the circle, they get out, and a fresh batch of people get in. Each one of these batches is like one of these manifestations, from the lowest animals to the highest man. Nature is like the chain of the Ferris Wheel, endless and infinite, and these little carriages are the bodies or forms in which fresh batches of souls are riding, going up higher and higher until they become perfect and come out of the wheel. But the wheel goes on. . . . There is no motion in a straight line. Everything moves in a circle; a straight line, infinitely produced, becomes a circle. If that is the case, there cannot be eternal degeneration for any soul. It cannot be. Everything must complete the circle, and come back to its source. What are you and I and all these souls? . . . You and I must be part of the cosmic consciousness, cosmic life, cosmic mind, which got involved, and we must complete the circle and go back to this cosmic intelligence which is God.

— *Vivekananda*

Ferris Wheel: "An amusement device consisting of a giant power-driven steel wheel, revolvable on its stationary axle, and carrying a number of balanced passenger cars around its rim" — G. Webster W. G. Ferris erected the first of its kind for the Chicago Exposition of 1893. This Ferris Wheel was 264 feet high and powered by two reversible 2,000 horsepower engines. Its axle was 45 feet long,weighed 56 tons, and was the largest steel forging ever made. The wheel could carry 60 passengers in each of the 36 coaches, and took twenty minutes for a complete revolution. It cost $362,000 but earned money for its owners as well as for the Exposition.

Katherine Abbot Sanborn

Breezy Meadows, Metcalf, Massachusetts

Vivekananda was disappointed when he learned that the Parliament of Religions would not open till the second week of September and that no one would be admitted without proper references.

He had learned that Boston was the Athens of America and also that it was much less expensive than Chicago. So after staying in Chicago for twelve days, most of which he had spent at the Fair, he took the train to Boston.

Previously, while travelling from Vancouver to Chicago, he had met Miss Katherine Abbot Sanborn, a distinguished woman of Boston. Attracted by Swamiji's noble bearing, she had approached and entered into conversation with him. She was more than interested to know that he was a Hindu monk and had come to America to preach the truths of Vedanta. When they parted Kate Sanborn gave her address [Breezy Meadows, Metcalf, Massachusetts] to the swami and informed him that she knew men and women of learning and culture to whom she would be glad to introduce him.

JUST NOW I AM LIVING AS THE GUEST of an old lady in a village near Boston. I accidentally made her acquaintance in the railway train, and she invited me to come over and live with her. I have an advantage in living with her, in saving for some time my expenditure of £1 per day, and she has the advantage of inviting her friends over here and showing them a curio from India! And all this must be borne. Starvation, cold, hooting in the streets on account of my quaint dress, these are what I have to fight against. But, my dear boy, no great things were ever done without great labour.

— *Vivekananda*

Professor John Henry Wright

Mary Tappan Wright

Kate Sanborn had a Hindoo monk in tow as I believe I mentioned in my last letter. John went down to meet him in Boston and missing him, invited him up here. He came Friday! In a long saffron robe that caused universal amazement. He was a most gorgeous vision. He had a superb carriage of the head, was very handsome in an oriental way, about thirty years old in time, ages in civilization. He stayed until Monday and was one of the most interesting people I have yet come across. We talked all and day all night and began again with interest the next morning. The town was in a fume to see him; the boarders at Miss Lane's in wild excitement. They were in and out of the Lodge [the Wright's cottage] constantly and little Mrs. Merill's eyes were blazing and her cheeks red with excitement. Chiefly we talked religion. It was a kind of revival. I have not felt so wrought up for a long time myself!

— *Mary Tappan Wright, written to her mother, 29 August 1893*

THE SWAMI WAS ENCOURAGED BY PROFESSOR WRIGHT to represent Hinduism in the Parliament of Religions, since that was the only way he could be introduced to the nation at large. When he announced, however, that he had no credentials, the professor replied, "To ask you, swami, for your credentials is like asking the sun about its right to shine." He wrote about the swami to a number of important people connected with the Parliament, especially to the chairman of the committee on selection of delegates, who was one of his friends, and said, "Here is a man more learned than all our learned professors put together." Professor Wright bought the swami's railroad ticket for Chicago.

The Hale residence, 541 Dearborn Avenue, Chicago, which Swamiji made his headquarters

Mrs. George W. Hale

Most probably a couple of days before the commencement of the Parliament of Religions, Swamiji reached Chicago from Boston and to his dismay found that he had lost the address of the office which Professor Wright had given him. He made inquiries but none could help him. Moreover, because of his strange monk's robes and his travel-worn appearance, he was rudely treated at some houses. At last, exhausted, he sat down quietly upon the sidewalk, determined to abide by the will of God. At this moment, Mrs. George W. Hale came out from her residence, which was just opposite to where Swamiji was sitting, and asked him: "Sir, are you a delegate to the Parliament of Religions?" The swami told her his difficulties. Immediately she invited him into her house and afterwards she herself took him to the office of the Parliament of Religions.

The four cousins left to right: Harriet McKindley, Mary Hale, Isabelle McKindley, Harriet Hale

Swamiji often stayed with the Hales. He called Mr. Hale "Father Pope" and Mrs. Hale "Mother Church." Mrs. Hale's daughters, Mary and Harriet, and their cousins, Isabelle and Harriet McKindley, were his "sisters."

I am ever grateful to you four sisters; to you I owe everything in this country. May you be ever blessed and happy. Wherever I be, you will always be remembered with the deepest gratitude and the sincerest love. . . . You are all so kind, the whole family, to me, I must have belonged to you in the past, as we Hindus say.

I HAVE NEVER SEEN WOMEN ELSEWHERE as cultured and educated as they are here. . . . I have seen thousands of women here whose hearts are as pure and stainless as snow. Oh, how free they are! It is they who control social and civic duties. . . . Their kindness to me is immeasurable. Since I came here, I have been welcomed by them to their houses. They are providing me with food, arranging for my lectures, taking me to market, and doing everything for my comfort and convenience. I shall never be able to repay in the least the deep debt of gratitude I owe to them.

— *Vivekananda*

George W. Hale

Mr. John B. Lyon

Mrs. John B. Lyon

Cornelia Conger wrote in her reminiscences how her grandparents, Mr. and Mrs. John B. Lyon, received Swamiji as their guest. They were his official hosts during the Parliament of Religions.

When my grandfather woke up, she told him of the problem [the colour prejudice of their southern guests] and said he must decide whether it would be uncomfortable for Swami and for our southern friends to be together. If so, she said he could put Swami up as our guest at the new Auditorium Hotel near us. My grandfather was dressed about half an hour before breakfast and went into the library to read his morning paper. There he found Swami and, before breakfast was served, he came to my grandmother and said: "I don't care a bit, Emily, if all our guests leave! This Indian is the most brilliant and interesting man who has ever been in our home, and he shall stay as long as he wishes." That began a warm friendship between them which was later summed up — much to my grandfather's embarrassment — by having Swami calmly remark to a group of my grandfather's friends one day at the Chicago Club, "I believe Mr. Lyon is the most Christ-like man I ever met!"

ONCE HE [SWAMIJI] SAID TO MY GRANDMOTHER that he had had the greatest temptation of his life in America. She liked to tease him a bit and said, "Who is she, Swami?" He burst out laughing and said, "Oh, it is not a lady, it is Organization!" . . .

Swamiji was such a dynamic and attractive personality that many women were quite swept away by him and made every effort by flattery to gain his interest. He was still young, and, in spite of his great spirituality and his brilliance of mind, seemed to be very unworldly. This used to trouble my grandmother who feared he might be put in a false or uncomfortable position, and she tried to caution him a little. Her concern touched and amused him, and he patted her hand and said: "Dear Mrs. Lyon, you dear American mother of mine, don't be afraid for me. It is true I often sleep under a banyan tree with a bowl of rice given me by a kindly peasant, but it is equally true that I also am sometimes the guest in the palace of a great Maharaja and a slave girl is appointed to wave a peacock feather fan over me all night long! I am used to temptation, and you need not fear for me!"

Rev. John Henry Barrows, Chairman of the General Committee

Charles Carroll Bonney, President of the Parliament of Religions

It was the Reverend John Henry Barrows, pastor of the first Presbyterian Church of Chicago, who was Chairman of the General Committee and responsible for carrying out the elaborate preparations for the Parliament.

The work of the Committee was voluminous. More than 10,000 letters and 40,000 documents were sent out, and answers from all parts of the globe were received by the bushel. Barrows writes pridefully: "For thirty months nearly all the railroads and steamship lines of the world were unconsciously working for the Parliament of Religions. The post office clerks at Chicago handled great bundles of letters which had previously passed through the brown fingers of the postal clerks in Madras, Bombay and Tokyo." Advisory Councilors were selected from all parts of the world, their number finally reaching 3,000.

SWAMIJI WROTE: "THINK OF THAT MIND that planned and carried out with great success that gigantic undertaking, and he, no clergyman, a lawyer presiding over the dignitaries of all the churches, the sweet, learned, patient Mr. Bonney with all his soul speaking through his bright eyes. . . ." Bonney himself described his dream of what the Parliament might accomplish: "I became acquainted with the great religious systems of the world in my youth, and have enjoyed an intimate association with leaders of many churches during my maturer years. I was thus led to believe that if the great religious faiths could be brought into relations of friendly intercourse, many points of sympathy and union would be found, and the coming unity of mankind in the love of God and the service of man be greatly facilitated and advanced."

Vivekananda as a delegate to the Parliament of Religions (from an early print), September 1893

The Art Institute of Chicago, 1893

The historic and unprecedented Parliament of Religions was held in Chicago's newly-constructed and imposing Art Institute on Michigan Avenue. Here, during the seventeen days of the Parliament proper, assembled a great concourse of humanity, which included in its midst many of the most distinguished people of the world: the audience was sprinkled liberally with eminent men of every profession, many of the greatest philosophers of the West were in daily attendance, and among the delegates were high ecclesiastics of various faiths. The main sessions of the Parliament were held morning, afternoon and evening in the large Hall of Columbus, whose floor and gallery had a combined seating capacity of 4,000.

A noted American author wrote of the Parliament of Religions and of Swami Vivekananda:

Prior to the convention of the Parliament of Religions, adjunct to the World's Columbian Exposition in 1893, which was convened in Chicago, little was known of Vivekananda in this country. On that auspicious occasion, however, he appeared in all his magnificent grandeur. It was on Monday, 11 September at 10 a.m. . . . On that memorable . . . morning there sat upon the platform of the great Hall of Columbus representatives of the religious hopes and beliefs of twelve hundred millions of the human race. It was indeed impressive. In the centre sat Cardinal Gibbons, highest prelate of the Roman Catholic Church on the Western Continent. He was seated upon a Chair of State and opened the meeting with a prayer. On the right and left of him were gathered the Oriental delegates, whose brilliant attire vied with his own scarlet robes in brilliancy. Conspicuous among the followers of Brahma, Buddha and Mohammed was an eloquent monk from India, Vivekananda by name. He was clad in gorgeous red apparel and wore a large turban, his remarkably fine features and bronze complexion standing out prominently in the great throng.

Sister Nivedita wrote in the introduction of The Complete Works of Swami Vivekananda:

Others stood beside Swami Vivekananda, on the same platform as he, as apostles of particular creeds and churches. But it was his glory that he came to preach a religion to which each of these was, in his own words, "only a travelling, a coming up, of different men and women, through various conditions and circumstances to the same goal."

A view of the delegates at the Parliament of Religions

Hall of Columbus, Art Institute, Chicago, 1893

At the World's Parliament of Religions, Chicago, 11 September 1893:

RESPONSE TO WELCOME

Sisters and Brothers of America,

It fills my heart with joy unspeakable to rise in response to the warm and cordial welcome which you have given us. I thank you in the name of the most ancient order of monks in the world; I thank you in the name of the mother of religions; and I thank you in the name of the millions and millions of Hindu people of all classes and sects.

My thanks, also, to some of the speakers on this platform, who, referring to the delegates from the Orient, have told you that these men from far-off nations may well claim the honour of bearing to different lands the idea of toleration. I am proud to belong to a religion which has taught the world both tolerance and universal acceptance. We not only believe in universal toleration, but we accept all religions as true. I am proud to belong to a nation which has sheltered the persecuted and the refugees of all religions and all nations of the earth. I am proud to tell you that we have gathered in our bosom the purest remnant of the Israelites, who came to southern India and took refuge with us in the very year in which their holy temple was shattered by Roman tyranny. I am proud to belong to the religion which has sheltered and is still fostering the remnant of the grand Zoroastrian nation. I will quote to you, brethren, a few lines from a hymn that I remember to have repeated from my earliest boyhood, which is every day repeated by millions of human beings: "As the different streams having their sources in different places all mingle their water in the sea, so, O Lord, the different paths which men take through different tendencies, various though they appear, crooked or straight, all lead to Thee."

The present convention, which is one of the most august assemblies ever held, is in itself a vindication, a declaration to the world of the wonderful doctrine preached in the Gita: "Whosoever comes to Me, through whatsoever form, I reach him. All men are struggling through paths which in the end lead to Me." Sectarianism, bigotry, and its horrible descendant, fanaticism, have long possessed this beautiful earth. They have filled the earth with violence, drenched it often and often with human blood, destroyed civilization, and sent whole nations to despair. Had it not been for these horrible demons, human society would be far more advanced than it is now. But their time is come; and I fervently hope that the bell that tolled this morning in honour of this convention may be the death-knell of all fanaticism, of all persecutions with the sword or with the pen, and of all uncharitable feelings between persons wending their way to the same goal.

Chicago, September 1893

I addressed the assembly as "Sisters and Brothers of America," a deafening applause of two minutes followed, and then I proceeded; and when it was finished, I sat down, almost exhausted with emotion. The next day all the papers announced that my speech was the hit of the day, and I became known to the whole of America. . . .

You may wonder what made them do this, you may wonder if I had some strange power. Let me tell you that I did have a power and this is it — never once in my life did I allow myself to have even one sexual thought. I trained my mind, my thinking, and the powers that man usually uses along that line I put into a higher channel, and it developed a force so strong that nothing could resist it.

— *Vivekananda*

Responses of the newspapers and other individuals:

He is undoubtedly the greatest figure in the Parliament of Religions. After hearing him we feel how foolish it is to send missionaries to this learned nation.

— ***New York Herald***

Swami Vivekananda exercised a wonderful influence over his auditors.

— ***Rev. John H. Barrows, Chairman of the General Committee and the organizer of the Parliament***

But eloquent as were many of the brief speeches, no one expressed as well the spirit of the Parliament (of religions) and its limitations as the Hindu monk. I copy his address in full, but I can only suggest its effect upon the audience; for he is an orator by Divine right, and his strong intelligent face in its picturesque setting of yellow and orange was hardly less interesting than these earnest words and the rich rhythmical utterance he gave them.

. . . He speaks without notes, presenting his facts and his conclusions with the greatest art and the most convincing sincerity, and rising often to rich inspiring eloquence.

— ***New York Critique***

Chicago, September 1893

When that young man got up and said, "Sisters and Brothers of America," seven thousand people rose to their feet as a tribute to something they knew not what. When it was over I saw scores of women walking over the benches to get near him, and I said to myself, "Well, my lad, if you can resist that onslaught you are indeed a God!"

— ***Mrs. S. K. Blodgett***

He is a great favourite at the Parliament from the grandeur of his sentiments and his appearance as well. If he merely crosses the platform he is applauded; and this marked approval of thousands he accepts in a childlike spirit of gratification without a trace of conceit.

— ***Boston Evening Transcript***

From the day the wonderful professor [the swami] delivered his speech, which was followed by other addresses, he was followed by a crowd wherever he went. In going in and coming out of the building, he was daily beset by hundreds of women who almost fought with each other for a chance to get near him, and shake his hand.

— ***A contemporary newspaper***

The face and dress which attracted the most notice, especially from the ladies, was that of Swami Vivekananda, a young man exceptionally handsome and with features that would command attention anywhere. His dress was bright orange, and he wore a long coat and regulation turban of that color. Vivekananda is a Brahmin monk, and Prof. Wright of Harvard is quoted as saying that he is one of the best educated men in the world.

— ***Chicago Times***

In certain respects the most fascinating personality was the Brahmin monk, Swami Vivekananda with his flowing orange robe, saffron turban, smooth-shaven, shapely, handsome face, large, dark subtle penetrating eye, and with the air of one being inly-pleased with the consciousness of being easily master of his situation. His knowledge of English is as though it were his mother tongue.

— ***Chicago Advocate***

No religious body made so profound an impression upon the Parliament and the American people at large, as did Hinduism. . . . And by far the most important and typical representative of Hinduism was Swami Vivekananda, who, in fact, was beyond question the most popular and influential man in the Parliament.

— ***Merwin-Marie Snell, President of the Scientific Section of Columbian Exposition***

Some excerpts from the paper on **Hinduism** *read by Swami Vivekananda at the Parliament on 19 September 1893:*

The Hindus have received their religion through revelation, the Vedas. They hold that the Vedas are without beginning and without end. It may sound ludicrous to this audience that a book can be without beginning or end. But by the Vedas no books are meant. They mean the accumulated treasure of spiritual laws discovered by different persons in different times. Just as the law of gravitation existed before its discovery, and would exist if all humanity forgot it, so is it with the laws that govern the spiritual world. The moral, ethical, and spiritual relations between soul and soul and between individual spirits and the Father of all spirits, were there before their discovery, and would remain even if we forgot them.

The discoverers of these laws are called Rishis, and we honour them as perfected beings. I am glad to tell this audience that some of the very greatest of them were women.

❧ ❧ ❧

The Hindu believes that he is Spirit. Him the sword cannot pierce, him the fire cannot burn, him the water cannot melt, him the air cannot dry. The Hindu believes that every soul is a circle whose circumference is nowhere, but whose centre is located in the body, and that death means the change of this centre from body to body. The soul is not bound by the conditions of matter. In its very essence it is free, unbounded, holy, pure, and perfect.

❧ ❧ ❧

A Vedic sage . . . proclaimed the glad tidings: "Hear, ye children of immortal bliss, even ye that reside in higher spheres! I have found the Ancient One who is beyond all darkness, all delusion. By knowing Him alone will you be saved from death over again." "Children of immortal bliss" — what a sweet, what a hopeful name! Allow me to call you, brethren, by that sweet name — heirs of immortal bliss. Yea, the Hindu refuses to call you sinners. Ye are the children of God, the sharers of immortal bliss, holy and perfect beings. Ye divinities on earth — sinners! It is a sin to call a man so; it is a standing libel on human nature. Come up, O lions, and shake off the delusion that you are

Chicago, September 1893
"It [the Parliament of Religions] has shown that every religion can make a stand in the world of thought, and has set people to thinking that the Lord is working everywhere." — Vivekananda

sheep. You are souls immortal, spirits free, blest and eternal. You are not matter, you are not bodies; matter is your servant, not you the servants of matter.

Science is nothing but the finding of unity. As soon as science reaches perfect unity, it will stop from further progress, because it will have reached the goal. Thus Chemistry cannot progress farther when it discovers one element out of which all others are made. Physics will stop when it is able to fulfill its services in discovering one energy of which all the others are but manifestations. And the science of religion will become perfect when it discovers Him who is the one Life in a universe of death, who is the constant basis of an ever-changing world, One who is the only Soul, of whom all souls are but delusive manifestations. Thus it is, through multiplicity and duality, that the ultimate unity is reached. Religion can go no farther. This, too, is the goal of all science.

Unity in variety is the plan of nature, and the Hindu has recognized it. Every other religion lays down certain fixed dogmas, and tries to force society to adopt them. It places before society only one coat which must fit Jack and John and Henry, all alike. If it does not fit John or Henry, he must go without a coat to cover his body. The Hindus have discovered that the Absolute can only be realized, or thought of, or stated, through the relative, and that the images, crosses, and crescents are simply so many symbols, so many pegs to hang spiritual ideas on. It is not that this help is necessary for everyone; but those that do not need it have no right to say that it is wrong. Nor is it compulsory in Hinduism.

One thing I must tell you. Idolatry in India does not mean anything horrible. . . . Man is to become divine by realizing the divine. Idols or temples or churches or books are only the supports, the helps, of his spiritual childhood; but on and on he must progress. He must not stop anywhere. "External worship, material worship," say the Hindu scriptures, "is the lowest stage; struggling to rise higher, through mental prayer, is the next stage; but the highest stage is when the Lord has been realized."

Mark that the same earnest man who is kneeling before the idol tells you: "Him the sun cannot express, nor the moon, nor the stars; the lightning cannot express Him, not to speak of fire. Through Him they shine." But he does not abuse anyone's idol or call its worship sin. He recognizes in it a necessary stage of life. "The child is father of the man." Would it be right for an old man to say that childhood is a sin or youth a sin?

If a man can realize his divine nature with the help of an image, would it be right to call that a sin? Or even when he has passed that stage, should he call it an error? To the Hindu, man is not travelling from error to truth, but from truth to truth — from lower to higher truth.

It is the same light coming through glasses of different colours. And these little variations are necessary for purposes of adaptation. But in the heart of everything the same truth reigns. The Lord has declared to the Hindu, in His incarnation as Krishna: "I am in every religion, like the thread through a string of pearls. Wherever thou seest extraordinary holiness and extraordinary power raising and purifying humanity, know thou that I am there." And what has been the result? I challenge the world to find, throughout the whole system of Sanskrit philosophy, any such expression as that the Hindu alone will be saved and not others. Says Vyasa, "We find perfect men also beyond the pale of our caste and creed." . . .

Hail, Columbia, motherland of liberty! It has been given to thee, who never dipped thy hand in thy neighbour's blood, who never found out that the shortest way of becoming rich was by robbing one's neighbours — it has been given to thee to march at the vanguard of civilization with the flag of harmony.

Chicago, September 1893

At the World's Parliament of Religions, Chicago, 15 September 1893:

WHY WE DISAGREE

I will tell you a little story. You have heard the eloquent speaker who has just finished say, "Let us cease from abusing each other," and he was very sorry that there should always be so much variance.

But I think I should tell you a story which will illustrate the cause of this variance. A frog lived in a well. It had lived there for a long time. It was born there and brought up there, and yet it was a little, small frog. Of course the evolutionists were not there then to tell us whether the frog lost its eyes or not, but, for our story's sake, we must take it for granted that it had eyes, and that every day it cleansed the water of all the worms and bacilli that lived there, with an energy that would do credit to our modern bacteriologists. In this way it went on and became a little sleek and fat. Well, one day another frog that lived in the sea came and fell into the well.

"Where are you from?"

"I am from the sea."

"The sea! How big is that? Is it as big as my well?" And it took a leap from one side of the well to the other.

Vivekananda on the platform of the Parliament

"My friend," said the frog of the sea, "how can you compare the sea with your little well?"

Then the frog took another leap and asked, "Is your sea so big?"

"What nonsense you speak, to compare the sea with your well!"

"But," said the frog of the well, "nothing can be bigger than my well; there can be nothing bigger than this. This fellow is a liar, so turn him out."

That has been the difficulty all the while.

I am a Hindu. I am sitting in my own little well and thinking that the whole world is my little well. The Christian sits in his little well and thinks the whole world is his well. The Mohammedan sits in his little well and thinks that is the whole world. I have to thank you of America for the great attempt you are making to break down the barriers of this little world of ours, and I hope that in the future the Lord will help you to accomplish your purpose.

— *Vivekananda*

A STRIKING FIGURE, CLAD IN YELLOW and orange, shining like the sun of India in the midst of the heavy atmosphere of Chicago, a lion head, piercing eyes, mobile lips, movements swift and abrupt — such was my first impression of Swami Vivekananda, as I met him in one of the rooms set apart for the use of the delegates to the Parliament of Religions. Monk, they called him, not unwarrantably, warrior-monk was he, and the first impression was of the warrior rather than of the monk, for he was off the platform, and his figure was instinct with pride of country, pride of race — the representative of the oldest of living religions. . . .

On the platform another side came out. The dignity and the inborn sense of worth and power still were there, but all was subdued to the exquisite beauty of the spiritual message which he had brought, to the sublimity of that matchless evangel of the East

East Indian group at Chicago, 1893. Left to right: *Narasimhacharya, Lakshminarayan, Vivekananda, H. Dharmapala and Virchand Gandhi*

which is the heart, the life of India, the wondrous teaching of the Self. Enraptured, the huge multitude hung upon his words; not a syllable must be lost, not a cadence missed! "That man a heathen!" said one, as he came out of the great hall, "and we send missionaries to his people! It would be more fitting that they should send missionaries to us."

— *Dr. Annie Besant*

AT THE PARLIAMENT OF RELIGIONS they used to keep Vivekananda until the end of the programme to make people stay until the end of the session. On a warm day, when a prosy speaker talked too long and people began going home by hundreds, the Chairman would get up and announce that Swami Vivekananda would give a short address just before the benediction. Then he would have the peaceable hundreds perfectly in tether. The four thousand fanning people in the Hall of Columbus would sit smiling and expectant, waiting for an hour or two of other men's speeches, to listen to Vivekananda for fifteen minutes. The Chairman knew the old rule of keeping the best until last.

— *Boston Evening Transcript*

Scene at the Parliament on the evening of the last day, 27 September 1893. (Vivekananda, second row, left of centre)

An excerpt from Vivekananda's address at the final session, 27 September 1893:

Much has been said of the common ground of religious unity. I am not going just now to venture my own theory. . . . The seed is put in the ground, and earth and air and water are placed around it. Does the seed become the earth, or the air, or the water? No. It becomes a plant, it develops after the law of its own growth, assimilates the air, the earth, and the water, converts them into plant substance, and grows into a plant.

Similar is the case with religion. The Christian is not to become a Hindu or a Buddhist, nor a Hindu or a Buddhist to become a Christian. But each must assimilate the spirit of the others and yet preserve his individuality and grow according to his own law of growth.

If the Parliament of Religions has shown anything to the world, it is this: It has proved to the world that holiness, purity, and charity are not the exclusive possessions of any church in the world, and that every system has produced men and women of the most exalted character. In the face of this evidence, if anybody dreams of the exclusive survival of his own religion and the destruction of the others, I pity him from the bottom of my heart, and point out to him that upon the banner of every religion will soon be written, in spite of resistance: "Help and not Fight," "Assimilation and not Destruction," "Harmony and Peace and not Dissension."

His [Vivekananda's] words are great music, phrases in the style of Beethoven, stirring rhythms like the march of Handel choruses. I cannot touch these sayings of his, scattered as they are through the pages of books at thirty years' distance, without receiving a thrill through my body like an electric shock. And what shocks, what transports must have been produced when in burning words they issued from the lips of the hero!

— *Romain Rolland* ❧

V

"I Have a Message to the West"

After his great success at the Parliament of Religions, Vivekananda joined a lecture bureau, which arranged for him a lecture tour all over the Midwest. Later he found that he was being cheated by the bureau, so he severed his contract with it. The American media made him well-known; as a result, he received invitations to lecture from various organizations. On 30 December 1894 Vivekananda said at the Brooklyn Ethical Society, "I have a message to the West, as Buddha had a message to the East."

What did Vivekananda teach in the West? He taught Vedanta, the universal philosophy and religion of the Upanishads, which originated thousands of years ago in India. The Western audience heard something new in his message: Sectarianism, bigotry, superstition, and intolerance were swept aside to make room for the harmony of all religions. It was an overwhelming message of goodwill and brotherly love.

"The swami had little patience with the constant harping on original sin in the West," wrote Cornelius Heijblom [later, Swami Atulananda]. "Why do you dwell on sin so much?" he exclaimed. "You are heirs of immortal bliss. We Hindus refuse to call you sinners! Ye are the children of God." "Thus the swami," wrote Heijblom, "cleared the theological atmosphere of the West. He sounded the trumpet call of glad tidings, of hope, of cheer, of salvation for all. And a new thought-wave swept over America. The swami brought the Gospel of the divinity of human beings.

"Swami Vivekananda had come to speak the truth, not to flatter the American nation to win their applause and sympathy. He had a great reverence for Christ and his teachings, but he saw the flaws in current Christianity. . . . In Detroit, before a large audience he exclaimed: 'I have come to make you better Christians. Remember Christ's saying, "Blessed are the peace-makers, for they shall be called the children of God." Everything that has selfishness for its basis must perish. If you want to live, go back to Christ. Go back to him who had nowhere to lay his head. Go back to him, and give up your vain pursuits. Better be ready to live in rags with Christ than to live in palaces without him.'"

Vivekananda redefined religion for his Western audience: "You must bear in mind that religion does not consist in talk, or doctrines or books, but in realization. It is not learning but *being*." "The old religions said that he was an atheist who did not believe in God. The new religion says that he is an atheist who does not believe in himself." "Religion is the idea which is raising the brute unto man, and man unto God. . . . Take religion from human society and what will remain? Nothing but a forest of brutes. Sense-happiness is not the goal of humanity. Wisdom is the goal of all life."

The supreme goal of human life, according to Vivekananda, is to manifest the divinity that is within all beings. How does one do it? Vivekananda described four paths, which he called yogas: karma yoga, the path of unselfish action; bhakti yoga, the path of devotion; jnana yoga, the path of knowledge; and raja yoga, the path of meditation. These yogas, or spiritual paths, help people to unite themselves with God. Thus they overcome all weaknesses and problems in their lives and attain supreme bliss and freedom.

Chicago, 1894. The handwriting on the picture: "When in search of knowledge or prosperity think that you would never have death or disease, and when worshipping God think that death's hand is in your hair." (Hitopadesha, introduction, 3)

The Himalayas, the place of ascetics

Shall we advise men to kneel down and cry, "O miserable sinners that we are!" No. Rather let us remind them of their divine nature. I will tell you a story. A lioness in search of prey came upon a flock of sheep, and as she jumped at one of them, she gave birth to a cub and died on the spot. The young lion was brought up in the flock, ate grass, and bleated like a sheep, and it never knew that it was a lion. One day another lion came across this flock and was astonished to see in it a huge lion eating grass and bleating like a sheep. At the sight of him the flock fled and the lion-sheep with them. But the lion watched his opportunity and one day found the lion-sheep asleep. He woke him up and said, "You are a lion." The other said, "No," and began to bleat like a sheep. But the stranger-lion took him to a lake and asked him to look in the water at his own image and see if it did not resemble him, the stranger-lion. He looked and acknowledged that it did. Then the stranger-lion began to roar and asked him to do the same. The lion-sheep tried his voice and was soon roaring as grandly as the other. And he was a sheep no longer.

That is it. We are lions in sheep's clothing of habit. We are hypnotized into weakness by our surroundings. And the province of Vedanta is the self-dehypnotization.

Strength, strength is what the Upanishads speak to me from every page. This is the one great thing to remember. It has been the one great lesson I have been taught in my life. Strength, it says, strength, O man, be not weak. Are there no human weaknesses? — says man. There are, say the Upanishads, but will more weakness heal them? Would you try to wash dirt with dirt? Will sin cure sin, weakness cure weakness? Strength, O man, strength, say the Upanishads. Stand up and be strong. Ay, it is the only literature in the world where you find the word *abhih*, "fearless," used again and again. In no other scripture in the world is this adjective applied either to God or to man. Abhih, [be] fearless! . . .

The Upanishads are the great mine of strength. Therein lies strength enough to invigorate the whole world. The whole world can be vivified, made strong, energized, through them. They will call with trumpet voice upon the weak, the miserable, and the downtrodden of all races, all creeds, and all sects to stand on their feet and be free. Freedom — physical freedom, mental freedom, and spiritual freedom are the watchwords of the Upanishads.

— *Vivekananda*

Chicago, September 1893

Chicago, September 1893

Each one thinks his method is best. Very good! But remember, it may be good for *you*. One food which is very indigestible to one is very digestible to another. Because it is good for you, do not jump to the conclusion that your method is everybody's method, that Jack's coat fits John and Mary. All the uneducated, uncultured, unthinking men and women have been put into that sort of straitjacket! Think for yourselves. Become atheists! Become materialists! That would be better. Exercise the mind! . . .

If you want to be religious, enter not the gate of any organized religions. They do a hundred times more evil than good, because they stop the growth of each one's individual development. Study everything, but keep your own seat firm. If you take my advice, do not put your neck into the trap. The moment they try to put their noose on you, get your neck out and go somewhere else. As the bee culling honey from many flowers remains free, not bound by any flower, be not bound. . . . Enter not the door of any organized religion. Religion is only between you and your God, and no third person must come between you. . . .

Here I can only lay before you what the Vedanta seeks to teach, and that is the deification of the world. The Vedanta does not in reality denounce the world. The ideal of renunciation nowhere attains such a height as in the teachings of the Vedanta. But, at the same time, dry suicidal advice is not intended; it really means deification of the world — giving up the world as we think of it, as we know it, as it appears to us — and to know what it really is. Deify it; it is God alone. We read at the commencement of one of the oldest of the Upanishads, "Whatever exists in this universe is to be covered with the Lord." . . .

You can have your wife; it does not mean that you are to abandon her, but that you are to see God in the wife. Give up your children; what does that mean? To turn them out of doors, as some human brutes do in every country? Certainly not. That is diabolism; it is not religion. But see God in your children. So, in everything. In life and in death, in happiness and in misery, the Lord is equally present. The whole world is full of the Lord. Open your eyes and see Him. This is what Vedanta teaches.

— *Vivekananda*

Temples or churches, books or forms, are simply the kindergarten of religion, to make the spiritual child strong enough to take higher steps; and these first steps are necessary if he wants religion. With the thirst, the longing for God, comes real devotion, real Bhakti. Who has the longing? That is the question. Religion is not in doctrines, in dogmas, nor in intellectual argumentation; it is being and becoming, it is realization. We hear so many talking about God and the soul, and all the mysteries of the universe, but if you take them one by one, and ask them, "Have you realized God? Have you seen your Soul?" — how many can say they have? And yet they are all fighting with one another! At one time, in India, representatives of different sects met together and began to dispute. One said that the only God was Shiva; another said, the only God was Vishnu, and so on; and there was no end to their discussion. A sage was passing that way, and was invited by the disputants to decide the matter. He first asked the man who was claiming Shiva as the greatest God: "Have you seen Shiva? Are you acquainted with Him? If not, how do you know He is the greatest God?" Then turning to the worshipper of Vishnu, he asked, "Have you seen Vishnu?" And after asking this question to all of them, he found out that not one of them knew anything of God. That was why they were disputing so much, for had they really known, they would not have argued. When a jar is being filled with water, it makes a noise, but when it is full, there is no noise. So, the very fact of these disputations and fighting among sects shows that they do not know anything about religion. Religion to them is a mere mass of frothy words, to be written in books. Each one hurries to write a big book, to make it as massive as possible, stealing his materials from every book he can lay his hands upon, and never acknowledging his indebtedness. Then he launches this book upon the world, adding to the disturbance that is already existing there.

Chicago, September 1893

When I began lecturing in Chicago and other cities, I had to deliver every week some twelve or fifteen or even more lectures at times. This excessive strain on the body and mind would exhaust me to a degree. I seemed to run short of subjects for lectures and was anxious where to find new topics for the morrow's lecture. New thoughts seemed altogether scarce. One day, after the lecture, I lay thinking of what means to adopt next. The thought induced a sort of slumber, and in that state I heard as if somebody standing by me was lecturing — many new ideas and new veins of thought, which I had scarcely heard or thought of in my life. On awaking I remembered them and reproduced them in my lecture. I cannot enumerate how often this phenomenon took place. Many, many days did I hear such lectures while lying in bed. Sometimes the lecture would be delivered in such a loud voice that the inmates of adjacent rooms would hear the sound and ask me the next day, "With whom, Swamiji, were you talking so loudly last night?" I used to avoid the question somehow. Ah, it was a wonderful phenomenon.

— *Vivekananda*

New York, 1895

The Vedantist says that a man is neither born nor dies nor goes to heaven, and that reincarnation is really a myth with regard to the soul. The example is given of a book being turned over. It is the book that evolves, not the man. Every soul is omnipresent, so where can it come or go? These births and deaths are changes in nature which we are mistaking for changes in us.

Reincarnation is the evolution of nature and the manifestation of the God within. . . .

We would describe the soul in these words: This soul the sword cannot cut, nor the spear pierce; the fire cannot burn nor water melt it; indestructible, omnipresent is this soul. . . .

I do not believe that there will come a time when all the evil in the world will vanish. How could that be? This stream goes on. Masses of water go out at one end, but masses are coming in at the other end.

The Vedanta says that you are pure and perfect, and that there is a state beyond good and evil, and that is your own nature. It is higher even than good. Good is only a lesser differentiation than evil.

We have no theory of evil. We call it ignorance.

So far as it goes, all dealing with other people, all ethics, is in the phenomenal world. As a most complete statement of truth, we would not think of applying such things as ignorance to God. Of Him we say that He is Existence, Knowledge, and Bliss Absolute. Every effort of thought and speech will make the Absolute phenomenal and break Its character.

There is one thing to be remembered: that the assertion — I am God — cannot be made with regard to the sense-world. If you say in the sense-world that you are God, what is to prevent your doing wrong? So the affirmation of your divinity applies only to the noumenal. If I am God, I am beyond the tendencies of the senses and will not do evil. . . .

All the criticism against the Advaita philosophy can be summed up in this, that it does not conduce to sense-enjoyments; and we are glad to admit that.

The Vedanta system begins with tremendous pessimism, and ends with real optimism. We deny the sense-optimism but assert the real optimism of the Super-sensuous. That real happiness is not in the senses but above the senses; and it is in every man. The sort of optimism which we see in the world is what will lead to ruin through the senses.

Abnegation has the greatest importance in our philosophy. Negation implies affirmation of the Real Self. The Vedanta is pessimistic so far as it negates the world of the senses, but it is optimistic in its assertion of the real world.

The Vedanta recognizes the reasoning power of man a good deal, although it says there is something higher than intellect; but the road lies through intellect.

We need reason to drive out all the old superstitions; and what remains is Vedantism. There is a beautiful Sanskrit poem in which the sage says to himself: "Why weepest thou, my friend? There is no fear nor death for thee. Why weepest thou? There is no misery for thee, for thou art like the infinite blue sky, unchangeable in thy nature. Clouds of all colours come before it, play for a moment, and pass away; it is the same sky. Thou hast only to drive away the clouds."...

The Vedanta teaches that Nirvana can be attained here and now, that we do not have to wait for death to reach it. Nirvana is the realization of the Self; and after having once known that, if only for an instant, never again can one be deluded by the mirage of personality.

Chicago, September 1893

Men in general lay all the blame of life on their fellow-men, or, failing that, on God, or they conjure up a ghost, and say it is fate. Where is fate, and who is fate? We reap what we sow. We are the makers of our own fate. . . .

Therefore, blame none for your own faults, stand upon your own feet, and take the whole responsibility upon yourselves. Say, "This misery that I am suffering is of my own doing, and that very thing proves that it will have to be undone by me alone." That which I created, I can demolish; that which is created by someone else I shall never be able to destroy. Therefore, stand up, be bold, be strong. Take the whole responsibility on your own shoulders, and know that you are the creator of your own destiny. All the strength and succour you want is within yourselves. Therefore, make your own future. "Let the dead past bury its dead." The infinite future is before you, and you must always remember that each word, thought, and deed, lays up a store for you and that as the bad thoughts and bad works are ready to spring upon you like tigers, so also there is the inspiring hope that the good thoughts and good deeds are ready with the power of a hundred thousand angels to defend you always and forever.

"This Atman is first to be heard of." Hear day and night that you are that Soul. Repeat it to yourselves day and night till it enters into your very veins, till it tingles in every drop of blood, till it is in your flesh and bone. Let the whole body be full of that one ideal, "I am the birthless, the deathless, the blissful, the omniscient, the omnipotent, ever-glorious Soul." Think on it day and night; think on it till it becomes part and parcel of your life. Meditate upon it, and out of that will come work. "Out of the fullness of the heart the mouth speaketh," and out of the fullness of the heart the hand worketh also. Action will come. Fill yourselves with the ideal; whatever you do, think well on it. All your actions will be magnified, transformed, deified, by the very power of the thought. If matter is powerful, thought is omnipotent. Bring this thought to bear upon your life, fill yourselves with the thought of your almightiness, your majesty, and your glory. . . .

These are sometimes terrible doctrines to teach. I know people who get frightened at these ideas, but for those who want to be practical, this is the first thing to learn. Never tell yourselves or others that you are weak. Do good if you can, but do not injure the world.

I have a message to give, I have no time to be sweet to the world, and every attempt at sweetness makes me a hypocrite. I will die a thousand deaths rather than lead a jelly-fish existence and yield to every requirement of this foolish world, no matter whether it be my own country or a foreign country. . . .

The accommodating man finds a path of roses; the non-accommodating, one of thorns. But the worshippers of "Vox populi" go to annihilation in a moment; the children of truth live forever. . . .

"Youth and beauty vanish, life and wealth vanish, name and fame vanish, even the mountains crumble into dust. Friendship and love vanish. Truth alone abides." God of Truth, be Thou alone my guide!

— *Vivekananda*

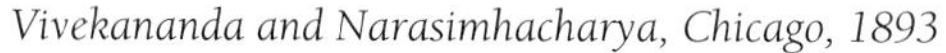

Vivekananda and Narasimhacharya, Chicago, 1893

New York, 1895

Life will be a desert, human life will be vain, if we cannot know the beyond. It is very good to say: Be contented with the things of the present moment. The cows and the dogs are, and so are all animals, and that is what makes them animals. So if man rests content with the present and gives up all search into the beyond, mankind will all have to go back to the animal plane again. It is religion, this inquiry into the beyond, that makes the difference between man and an animal. . . .

Can religion really bring bread and clothes? It does. It is always doing so, and it does infinitely more than that; it brings to man eternal life. It has made man what he is, and will make of this human animal a God. That is what religion can do. Take off religion from human society, what will remain? Nothing but a forest of brutes.

It is one of the evils of your Western civilization that you are after intellectual education alone, and take no care of the heart. It only makes men ten times more selfish, and that will be your destruction. When there is conflict between the heart and the brain, let the heart be followed, because intellect has only one state, reason, and within that, intellect works, and cannot get beyond. It is the heart which takes one to the highest plane, which intellect can never reach; it goes beyond intellect, and reaches to what is called inspiration. . . . Through the intellect is not the way to solve the problem of misery, but through the heart. If all this vast amount of effort had been spent in making men purer, gentler, more forbearing, this world would have a thousandfold more happiness than it has today. Always cultivate the heart; through the heart the Lord speaks and through the intellect you yourself speak.

— *Vivekananda*

Vivekananda taught at the Green Acre summer conferences in the summer of 1894. He wrote to the Hale Sisters on 31 July 1894:

This is a big inn and farm-house where the Christian Scientists are holding a session. . . . The other night the camp people went to sleep beneath a pine tree under which I sit every morning à la Hindu and talk to them. Of course I went with them, and we had a nice night under the stars, sleeping on the lap of mother earth, and I enjoyed every bit of it. I cannot describe to you that night's glories — after a year of brutal life that I have led, to sleep on the ground, to meditate under the tree in the forest! The inn people are more or less well-to-do, and the camp people are healthy, young, *sincere*, and holy men and women. I teach them Shivoham, Shivoham [I am Shiva], and they all repeat it, innocent and pure as they are and brave beyond all bounds. And so I am happy and glorified. Thank God for making me poor, thank God for making these children in the tents poor. The Dudes and Dudines are in the Hotel, but iron-bound nerves and souls of triple steel and spirits of fire are in the camp. If you had seen them yesterday, when the rain was falling in torrents and the cyclone was overturning everything, hanging by their tent strings to keep them from being blown down, and standing on the majesty of their souls — these brave ones — it would have done your hearts good. I will go a hundred miles to see the like of them. Lord bless them! . . .

Stick to God! Who cares what comes to the body or to anything else! Through the terrors of evil, say — my God, my love! Through the pangs of death, say — my God, my love! Through all the evils under the sun, say — my God, my love! Thou art here, I see Thee. Thou art with me, I feel Thee. I am Thine, take me. I am not of the world's but Thine, leave not then me. Do not go for glass beads leaving the mine of diamonds! This life is a great chance. What, seekest thou the pleasures of the world? — He is the fountain of all bliss. Seek for the highest, aim at that highest, and you *shall* reach the highest.

Vivekananda and Mrs. Ole Bull, Ridgely Manor, October 1899

A group at Green Acre, Maine, 1894

Green Acre, 1894

Green Acre, 1894

Each soul is potentially divine.The goal is to manifest this Divinity within by controlling nature, external and internal.

Do this either by work, or worship, or psychic control, or philosophy — by one, or more, or all of these — and be free.

This is the whole of religion. Doctrines, or dogmas, or rituals, or books, or temples, or forms, are but secondary details.

I have been asked many times, "Why do you laugh so much and make so many jokes?" I become serious sometimes — when I have stomach-ache! The Lord is all blissfulness. He is the reality behind all that exists, He is the goodness, the truth in everything. You are His incarnations. That is what is glorious. The nearer you are to Him, the less you will have occasions to cry or weep. The further we are from Him, the more will long faces come. The more we know of Him, the more misery vanishes. If one who lives in the Lord becomes miserable, what is the use of living in Him? What is the use of such a God? Throw Him overboard into the Pacific Ocean! We do not want Him!

— Vivekananda

ONE MORNING BEFORE BREAKFAST SWAMIJI came out from his room with a Sanskrit Gita in his hand. I [Josephine MacLeod] was behind him. Seeing me, he said, "Joe, I am going to sit under that pine (pointing to a nearby pine) and read the Bhagavad Gita. See that the breakfast is sumptuous today." Half an hour later I went over to the pine tree and saw Swamiji sitting there motionless. The Gita had fallen from his hand and the front of his robe was wet with tears.

I went nearer and saw that his breathing had stopped altogether. I trembled in fear — Swamiji must

Green Acre, 1894. Left to right: *Vivekananda, Sarah Farmer, M. H. Gulisian of Armenia, Edward Everett Hale.*

Vivekananda, Sarah Farmer (seated to his right), Charles Malloy (standing, white hat and cane) and others in the pines at Green Acre, 1894

be dead. I did not shout, but ran to Francis Leggett and told him, "Come quick, Swami Vivekananda has left us." My sister [Betty] ran to the spot with loud cries and my [future] brother-in-law also came with tears in his eyes. By now seven or eight minutes had passed. Swamiji was still in the same position. But my brother-in-law said, "He is in a trance; I will shake him out of it." I stopped him, shouting, "Never do that!" I remembered that Swamiji had said once that when he would be in deep meditation one should not touch him. Another five minutes or so passed, then we saw the signs of breathing. His eyes had been half closed; now slowly they opened. And then Swamiji, as if soliloquizing, said, "Who am I, where am I?" Thrice he spoke like that, and then, wide awake, he saw us, was very much embarrassed, stood up, and said: "I am sorry to have frightened you all. But I have this state of consciousness now and then. I shall not leave my body in your country. Betty, I am hungry, let's hurry."

— *Josephine MacLeod*

Camp Percy, New Hampshire, June 1895. Vivekananda went into nirvikalpa samadhi along this path where it winds farther along the shore of Lake Christine.

WEDNESDAY, 19 JUNE 1895

This day marks the beginning of the regular teaching given daily by Swami Vivekananda to his disciples at Thousand Island Park on the St. Lawrence River, New York State. He opened the Bible at the Book of John, saying that since the students were all Christians, it was proper that he should begin with the Christian scriptures.

"In the beginning was the Word, and the Word was with God, and the Word was God." The Hindu calls this maya, the manifestation of God, because it is the power of God. The Absolute reflecting through maya is what we call nature. The Word has two manifestations: the general one of nature, and the special one of the great Incarnations of God — Krishna, Buddha, Jesus, and Ramakrishna. Christ, the special manifestation of the Absolute, is known and knowable. The Absolute cannot be known. We cannot know the Father; we can only know the Son. We can only see the Absolute through the "Tint of humanity," through Christ.

In the first five verses of John is the whole essence of Christianity; each verse is full of the profoundest philosophy. . . .

"Blessed are the pure in heart, for they shall see God." This sentence alone would save mankind if all the books and prophets were lost. This purity of heart will bring the vision of God. It is the theme of the whole music of this universe. In purity there is no bondage. When we remove the veil of ignorance by purity, then we manifest ourselves as we really are and know that we were never in bondage. The seeing of many is the great sin of all the world. See all as the Self and love all; let all ideas of separateness go.

Vivekananda Cottage at Thousand Island Park, New York. (The open upper window in the left wing belongs to Vivekananda's room. The upper porch was where the evening talks were given, and the swami's seat was at the end near his room. The morning instruction embodied in Inspired Talks was given in the room to the left of the lower porch.)

WEDNESDAY, 7 AUGUST 1895

The last day has been a very wonderful and precious one. This morning there was no class. He [Swamiji] asked C. [Christine] and me [Mary Funke] to take a walk, as he wished to be alone with us. (The others had been with him all summer, and he felt we should have a last talk.) We went up a hill about half a mile away. All was woods and solitude. Finally he selected a low-branched tree, and we sat under the low-spreading branches. Instead of the expected talk, he suddenly said: "Now we will meditate. We shall be like Buddha under the Bo-tree." He seemed to turn to bronze, so still was he. Then a thunderstorm came up, and it poured. He never noticed it. I raised my umbrella and protected him as much as possible. Completely absorbed in his meditation, he was oblivious of everything. Soon we heard shouts in the distance. The others had come out after us with raincoats and umbrellas. Swamiji looked around regretfully, for we *had* to go, and said, "Once more am I in Calcutta in the rains."

— *Mary Funke*

Vivekananda Oak and Rock at Thousand Island Park. He had samadhi here.

Thousand Island Park, 1895

In the world, take always the position of the giver. Give everything and look for no return. Give love, give help, give service, give any little thing you can, but keep out barter. Make no conditions, and none will be imposed. Let us give out of our own bounty, just as God gives to us.

NEITHER SEEK NOR AVOID. Take what comes. It is liberty to be affected by nothing. Do not merely endure — be unattached.

RELIGION WITHOUT PHILOSOPHY runs into superstition. Philosophy without religion becomes dry atheism.

RELIGION, THE GREAT MILCH COW, has given many kicks, but never mind — it also gives a great deal of milk. The milkman does not mind the kick of the cow which gives much milk.

EVEN IF THERE BE NO GOD, still hold fast to love. It is better to die seeking God than to live as a dog, seeking only carrion. Choose the highest ideal and give your life up to that. "Death being so certain, it is the highest thing to give up life for a great purpose."

RELIGION GIVES YOU NOTHING NEW. It only takes off obstacles and lets you see your Self.

DO NOT CLING TO OLD SUPERSTITIONS. Be ever ready for new truths. "Fools are they who would drink brackish water from a well that their forefathers have dug and would not drink pure water from a well that others have dug." Until we realize God for ourselves we can know nothing about Him. How can we understand that Moses saw God unless we too see Him? If God ever came to anyone He will come to me. I will go to God direct. Let Him talk to me. I cannot take belief as a basis — that is atheism and blasphemy. If God spoke to a man in the deserts of Arabia two thousand years ago, He can also speak to me today, else how can I know that He has not died?

THINK DAY AND NIGHT: "This universe is zero. Only God is." Have intense desire to get free. Say, "Soham, Soham" [I am He, I am He], whatever comes. Let the body die. This idea of the body is but a worn-out fable. Be still and know that you are God.

— *Vivekananda*

Thousand Island Park, 1895

I have found nothing that gives a better answer and a clearer explanation to the various vital questions which arise in a man's mind than the Vedanta philosophy so ably taught by the Swami Vivekananda.

Not only were his words in classroom and lecture-room those of instructive value, but also his conversations, while walking on the street or through Central Park [New York] always conveyed the one message. Many of our interesting little talks I can readily call to mind; for instance, on one occasion I expressed my regret to the swami that his sublime teachings had no larger following, and his wise and fitting answer was: "I could have thousands more at my lectures if I wanted them. It is the sincere student who will help to make this work a success and not merely the large audiences. If I succeed in my whole life to help one man to reach freedom, I shall feel that my labours have not been in vain, but quite successful." This remark filled me with the desire to be one of his students.

— *H. J. Van Haagen*

New York, 1895

"When the lotus opens, the bees come of their own accord to seek the honey; so let the lotus of your character be full-blown, and the results will follow." This is a great lesson to learn.

My Master taught me this lesson hundreds of times, yet I often forget it. Few understand the power of thought. If a man goes into a cave, shuts himself in, and thinks one really great thought and dies, that thought will penetrate the walls of that cave, vibrate through space, and at last permeate the whole human race. Such is the power of thought; be in no hurry therefore to give your thoughts to others. First have something to give. He alone teaches who has something to give, for teaching is not talking, teaching is not imparting doctrines, it is communicating. Spirituality can be communicated just as really as I can give you a flower. This is true in the most literal sense. . . .

I learned from my Master that the religions of the world are not contradictory or antagonistic. They are but various phases of one eternal religion. . . . In one man, religion is manifesting itself as intense activity, as work. In another, it is manifesting itself as intense devotion, in yet another, as mysticism, in others as philosophy, and so forth. It is wrong when we say to others, "Your methods are not right." Do not try to disturb the faith of any man.

— *Vivekananda*

In this world we find that all happiness is followed by misery as its shadow. Life has its shadow, death. They must go together, because they are not contradictory, not two separate existences, but different manifestations of the same unit — life and death, sorrow and happiness, good and evil. The dualistic conception that good and evil are two separate entities, and that they are both going on eternally, is absurd on the face of it. They are the diverse manifestations of one and the same fact, one time appearing as bad, and at another time as good. The difference does not exist in kind, but only in degree. They differ from each other in degree of intensity.

We find, as a matter of fact, that the same nerve systems carry good and bad sensations alike, and when the nerves are injured, neither sensation comes to us. The same phenomenon will produce pleasure in one and pain in another. The eating of meat produces pleasure in a man, but pain in the animal that is eaten. There has never been anything that gives pleasure to all alike. Some are pleased, others displeased. So on it will go.

London, 1895

London, 1895

THIS IS A WORLD OF GOOD AND EVIL. Wherever there is good, evil follows, but beyond and behind all these manifestations, all these contradictions, Vedanta finds that Unity. It says, "Give up what is evil and give up what is good." What remains then? Behind good and evil stands something that is yours, the real "you" — beyond every evil, and beyond every good too — and it is that which is manifesting itself as good and bad.

Know *that* first, and then, and then alone, will you be a true optimist, and not before; for then you will be able to control everything. Control these manifestations and you will be at liberty to manifest the real "you." First be master of yourself, stand up and be free, go beyond the pale of these laws. For these laws do not absolutely govern you; they are only part of your being. First, find out that you are not the slave of nature, never were and never will be — that this nature, infinite as you may think it, is only finite, a drop in the ocean, and your Soul is the ocean. You are beyond the stars, the sun, and the moon. They are like mere bubbles compared with your infinite being. Know that, and you will control both good and evil. Then alone will the whole vision change, and you will stand up and say, "How beautiful is good and how wonderful is evil!"

— *Vivekananda*

London, 1895

My ideal indeed can be put into a few words and that is: to preach unto mankind their divinity, and how to make it manifest in every movement of life.

One idea that I see clear as daylight is that misery is caused by *ignorance* and nothing else. Who will give the world light? Sacrifice in the past has been the Law, it will be, alas, for ages to come. The earth's bravest and best will have to sacrifice themselves for the good of many, for the welfare of all. Buddhas by the hundred are necessary with eternal love and pity.

Religions of the world have become lifeless mockeries. What the world wants is character. The world is in need of those whose life is one burning love, selfless. That love will make every word tell like thunderbolt.

Bold words and bolder deeds are what we want. Awake, awake, great ones! The world is burning with misery. Can you sleep?

LET US NOT BE CAUGHT THIS TIME. So many times maya has caught us, so many times have we exchanged our freedom for sugar dolls which melted when the water touched them.

Don't be deceived. Maya is a great cheat. Get out. Do not let her catch you this time. Do not sell your priceless heritage for such delusions. Arise, awake, stop not till the goal is reached.

Hold your money merely as a custodian for what is God's. Have no attachment for it. Let name and fame and money go; they are a terrible bondage. Feel the wonderful atmosphere of freedom. You are free, free, free! Oh blessed am I! Freedom am I! I am the Infinite! In my soul I can find no beginning and no end. All is my Self. Say this unceasingly.

I HAVE BEEN ASKED MANY TIMES how we can work if we do not have the passion which we generally feel for work. I also thought in that way years ago. But as I am growing older, getting more experience, I find it is not true. The less passion there is, the better we work. The calmer we are, the better for us and the more the amount of work we can do. When we let loose our feelings we waste so much energy, shatter our nerves, disturb our minds, and accomplish very little work. The energy that ought to have gone out as work is spent as mere feeling that counts for nothing. It is only when the mind is very calm and collected that the whole of its energy is spent in doing good work. And if you read the lives of the great workers the world has produced, you will find that they were wonderfully calm men. Nothing, as it were, could throw them off their balance. That is why the man who becomes angry never does a great amount of work, and the man whom nothing can make angry accomplishes so much. The man who gives way to anger or hatred or any other passion cannot work. He only breaks himself to pieces and does nothing practical. It is the calm, forgiving, equable, well-balanced mind that does the greatest amount of work.

London, 1895

THE QUESTION IS: IS RELIGION TO JUSTIFY itself by the discoveries of reason, through which every other science justifies itself? Are the same methods of investigation that we apply to sciences and knowledge outside, to be applied to the science of religion? In my opinion this must be so, and I am also of the opinion that the sooner it is done the better. If a religion is destroyed by such investigations, it was then all the time useless, unworthy superstition, and the sooner it goes the better. I am thoroughly convinced that its destruction would be the best thing that could happen. All that is dross will be taken off, no doubt, but the essential parts of religion will emerge triumphant out of this investigation. Not only will it be made scientific — as scientific, at least, as any of the conclusions of physics or chemistry — but it will have greater strength, because physics or chemistry has no internal mandate to vouch for its truth, which religion has.

London, December 1896

The religion of Vedanta can satisfy the demands of the scientific world in regard to the highest generalization and to the law of evolution. That the explanation of a thing comes from within itself is still more completely satisfied by Vedanta. . . .

The difference between man and man, between angels and man, between man and animals, between animals and plants, between plants and stones, is not in kind — because everyone, from the highest angel to the lowest particle of matter, is but an expression of that one infinite ocean — but the difference is only in degree. I am a low manifestation; you may be higher; but in both the materials are the same. . . .

No extraneous explanation is sought — none is asked for. The sum total of this whole universe is God Himself. Is God then matter? No, certainly not, for matter is that God perceived by the five senses. That God, as perceived through the intellect, is *mind*; and when the Spirit sees, He is seen as *Spirit*. He is not matter, but whatever is real in matter is He.

— *Vivekananda*

London, 1895

Meditation means the mind is turned back upon itself. The mind stops all the thought-waves and the world stops. Your consciousness expands. Every time you meditate you will keep your growth. . . . Work a little harder, more and more, and meditation comes. You do not feel the body or anything else. When you come out of it after an hour, you have had the most beautiful rest you ever had in your life. That is the only way you ever give rest to your system. Not even the deepest sleep will give you such rest as that. The mind goes on jumping even in deepest sleep. Just those few minutes in meditation your brain has almost stopped. Just a little vitality is kept up. You forget the body. You may be cut to pieces and not feel it at all. You feel such pleasure in it. You become so light. This perfect rest we will get in meditation.

THINK OF A SPACE IN YOUR HEART, and in the midst of that space think that a flame is burning. Think of that flame as your own soul and inside the flame is another effulgent light, and that is the Soul of your soul, God. Meditate upon that in the heart.

— *Vivekananda*

London, December 1896

Bhakti yoga is the science of higher love. It shows us how to direct it. It shows us how to control it, how to manage it, how to use it, how to give it a new aim, as it were, and from it obtain the highest and most glorious results — that is, how to make it lead us to spiritual blessedness. Bhakti yoga does not say, "Give up." It only says, "Love — love the Highest!" And everything low naturally falls off from him, the object of whose love is the Highest. . . .

We may represent love as a triangle, each of the angles of which corresponds to one of its inseparable characteristics. There can be no triangle without all its three angles, and there can be no true love without its three following characteristics: The first angle of our triangle of love is that love knows no bargaining. The second angle of the triangle of love is that love knows no fear. The third angle of the love-triangle is that love knows no rival, for in it is always embodied the lover's highest ideal.

❧ ❧ ❧

CONCENTRATION IS THE ESSENCE of all knowledge. Nothing can be done without it. Ninety percent of thought force is wasted by the ordinary human being, and therefore he is constantly committing blunders. The trained man, or mind, never makes a mistake. When the mind is concentrated and turned back on itself, all within us will be our servants, not our masters. The Greeks applied their concentration to the external world, and the result was perfection in art, literature, etc. The Hindus concentrated on the internal world, upon the unseen realms in the Self, and developed the science of yoga. Yoga is controlling the senses, will, and mind. The benefit of its study is that we learn to control instead of being controlled. The mind seems to be layer on layer. Our real goal is to cross all these intervening strata of our being and find God. The end and aim of yoga is to realize God.

— Vivekananda

London, December 1896

London, December 1896

My idea is that all religions are different forces in the economy of God, working for the good of mankind; and that not one can become dead, not one can be killed. Just as you cannot kill any force in nature, so you cannot kill any one of these spiritual forces. You have seen that each religion is living. . . .

Our watchword, then, will be acceptance, and not exclusion. Not only toleration, for so-called toleration is often blasphemy, and I do not believe in it. I believe in acceptance. Why should I tolerate? Toleration means that I think that you are wrong and I am just allowing you to live. Is it not a blasphemy to think that you and I are allowing others to live? I accept all religions that were in the past, and worship with them all; I worship God with every one of them, in whatever form they worship Him. I shall go to the mosque of the Mohammendan; I shall enter the Christian's church and kneel before the crucifix; I shall enter the Buddhistic temple, where I shall take refuge in Buddha and in his Law. I shall go into the forest and sit down in meditation with the Hindu, who is trying to see the Light which enlightens the heart of everyone.

Not only shall I do all these, but I shall keep my heart open for all that may come in the future. Is God's book finished? Or is it still a continuous revelation going on? It is a marvellous book — these spiritual revelations of the world. The Bible, the Vedas, the Koran, and all other sacred books are but so many pages, and an infinite number of pages remain yet to be unfolded. I would leave it open for all of them. We stand in the present, but open ourselves to the infinite future. We take in all that has been in the past, enjoy the light of the present, and open every window of the heart for all that will come in the future. Salutation to all the prophets of the past, to all the great ones of the present, and to all that are to come in the future!

— Vivekananda ❧

VI

East Meets West – I

From July 1893 to December 1896 Vivekananda travelled and lectured extensively in America and Europe. He met many distinguished men and women of the West, and tried to establish a bridge between the East and the West by removing social, religious, and cultural barriers. He emphasized in his lectures that the Truth is one and universal, and all human beings, knowingly or unknowingly, are marching towards It. In the realization of this oneness of Truth, people attain peace, bliss, and harmony.

"When we talk of East and West," writes Laura Glenn, an American writer, "we must remember one great fact that spirituality has no geographical limits. Truth is the same at all points of the compass: the law of gravitation does not function more in Europe than in Africa or Asia; the facts of chemistry are as true in an Indian as in a German laboratory; the heavens are as visible through a telescope in Tokyo as in Cambridge."

A knower of Truth is a universal person. He or she transcends all geographical, social, and religious barriers. Vivekananda experienced this Truth. He wrote to an Indian disciple from New York on 9 August 1895: "Every day my sight grows clearer. What is India, or England, or America to us? We are the servants of that God who by the ignorant is called Man. He who pours water at the root, does he not water the whole tree? . . . There is but one basis of well-being, social, political, or spiritual, to know that I and my brother are one. This is true for all countries and all people."

As a lover of humanity, Vivekananda voiced what was good for the West as well as the East. There was no motive, fear, or compromise in his message. Observing the materialistic civilization of the West, he said: "Materialism and all its miseries can never be conquered by materialism. Armies when they attempt to conquer armies only multiply and make brutes of humanity. Spirituality must conquer the West." In 1897, during one of his lectures, he said: "Europe, the centre of the manifestation of material energy, will crumble into dust within fifty years if she is not mindful to change her position, to shift her ground, and make spirituality the basis of her life. And what will save Europe is the religion of the Upanishad." The last two world wars were the proof of his prophecy.

Vivekananda had powerful insight. Like a good doctor, he could diagnose correctly and precisely the causes of the sufferings of a people as well as the degradation of a nation. On 18 November 1894 he wrote (from New York) to Raja Pyari Mohan Mukherji, a distinguished Indian: "I am thoroughly convinced that no individual or nation can live by holding itself apart from the community of others, and whenever such an attempt has been made under false ideas of greatness, policy, or holiness — the result has always been disastrous to the secluding one. . . . Give and take is the law; and if India wants to raise herself once more, it is absolutely necessary that she bring out her treasures and throw them broadcast among the nations of the earth, and in return be ready to receive what others have to give her. Expansion is life, contraction is death. Love is life, hatred is death." It is amazing how Vivekananda's letters from the West aroused the Indian nation and made him a patriot prophet.

Chicago, September 1893

Leon Landsberg (later, Swami Kripananda)
Drawing from the Detroit Free Press, *2 March 1896*

Nowhere in the world is to be found another nation like the Americans, so generous, broad-minded, hospitable, and so sincerely eager to accept new ideas. . . . There is no nation in the world so conservative as the English. They do not like so easily to accept any new idea, but if through perseverance they can be once made to understand any idea, they will never give it up by any means. Such firm determination you will find in no other nation. This is why they occupy the foremost position in the world in power and civilization.

In our country [India] there is only this religion of Vedanta. Compared with the Western civilization, it may be said, we have hardly got anything else. But by the preaching of this universal religion of Vedanta, a religion which gives equal rights to acquire spirituality to men of all creeds and all paths of religious practice, the civilized West would come to know what a wonderful degree of spirituality once developed in India and how that is still existing.

— *Vivekananda*

THE AMERICANS ARE A RECEPTIVE NATION. That is why the country is a hotbed of all kinds of religious and irreligious monstrosities. There is no theory so absurd, no doctrine so irrational, no claim so extravagant, no fraud so transparent, but can find their numerous believers and a ready market. To satisfy this craving, to feed the credulity of the people, hundreds of societies and sects are born for the salvation of the world, and to enable the prophets to pocket $25 to $100 initiation fees. Hobgoblins, spooks, mahatmas, and new prophets were rising every day. In this bedlam of religious cranks, the swami appeared to teach the lofty religion of the Vedas, the profound philosophy of Vedanta, the sublime wisdom of the ancient rishis. The most unfavourable environment for such a task!

— *Leon Landsberg*

John D. Rockefeller, ca. 1890

In Chicago Swamiji told John D. Rockefeller much of his past that was not known to any but himself, and made him understand that the money he had already accumulated was not his, that he was only a channel and that his duty was to do good to the world — that God had given him all his wealth in order that he might have an opportunity to help and do good to people.

Rockefeller was annoyed that anyone dared to talk to him that way and tell him what to do. He left the room in irritation, not even saying good-bye. But about a week after, again without being announced, he entered Swamiji's study and, finding him the same as before, threw on his desk a paper which told of his plans to donate an enormous sum of money toward the financing of a public institution.

"Well, there you are," he said. "You must be satisfied now, and you can thank me for it."

Swamiji didn't even lift his eyes, did not move. Then taking the paper, he quietly read it, saying, "It is for you to thank me." That was all. This was Rockefeller's first large donation to the public welfare.

IT WAS NO DOUBT ALSO IN Chicago that the swami first met the famous agnostic and orator Robert Ingersoll and more than once discussed religious and philosophical matters with him. During the course of these conversations the great agnostic cautioned the swami not to be too bold and outspoken, to be careful in his preaching of new doctrines and in his criticisms of the ways of life and thought of the people. When asked why, Mr. Ingersoll replied: "Fifty years ago you would have been hanged if you had come to preach in this country, or you would have been burned alive. You would have been stoned out of the villages if you had come even much later."

Ingersoll once said to me: "I believe in making the most out of this world, in squeezing the orange dry, because this world is all we are sure of." I replied: "I know a better way to squeeze the orange of this world than you do, and I get more out of it. I *know* I cannot die, so I am not in a hurry; I know there is no fear, so I enjoy the squeezing. I have no duty, no bondage of wife and children and property; I can love all men and women. Everyone is God to me. Think of the joy of loving man as God! Squeeze your orange this way and get ten thousandfold more out of it. Get every single drop."

— *Vivekananda*

Robert Ingersoll, an agnostic philosopher and orator

Harriet Monroe, an American poet, 1893

The Congress of Religions was a triumph for all concerned, especially for its generalissimo, the Reverend John H. Barrows, of Chicago's First Presbyterian Church, who had been preparing it for two years.

It was Swami Vivekananda, the magnificent, who stole the whole show and captured the town. . . . Others of the foreign groups spoke well, but the handsome monk in the orange robe gave us in perfect English a masterpiece. His personality, dominant, magnetic; his voice, rich as a bronze bell; the controlled fervor of his feeling; the beauty of his message to the Western world he was facing for the first time — these combined to give us a rare and perfect moment of supreme emotion. It was human eloquence at its highest pitch.

One cannot repeat a perfect moment — the futility of trying to has been almost a superstition with me. Thus I made no effort to hear Vivekananda speak again, during that autumn and winter when he was making converts by the score to his hope of uniting East and West in a world religion above the tumult of controversy.

— *Harriet Monroe*

Ella Wheeler Wilcox, an American poet, 1896

Before we had been ten minutes in the audience [New York, May 1895], we felt ourselves lifted up into an atmosphere so rarefied, so vital, so wonderful, that we sat spellbound and almost breathless to the end of the lecture. When it was over we went out with new courage, new hope, new strength, new faith, to meet life's daily vicissitudes. . . . It was that terrible winter of financial disasters, when banks failed and stocks went down like broken balloons, and businessmen walked through the dark valleys of despair, and the whole world seemed topsy-turvy. Sometimes after sleepless nights of worry and anxiety, my husband would go with me to hear the swami lecture, and then he would come out into the winter gloom and walk down the street smiling and say: "It is all right. There is nothing to worry over." And I would go back to my own duties and pleasures with the same uplifted sense of soul and enlarged vision. . . . "I do not come to convert you to a new belief," he said. "I want you to keep your own belief; I want to make the Methodist a better Methodist, the Presbyterian a better Presbyterian, the Unitarian a better Unitarian. I want to teach you to live the truth, to reveal the light within your own soul." He gave the message that strengthened the man of business, that caused the frivolous society woman to pause and think; that gave the artist new aspirations; that imbued the wife and mother, the husband and father, with a larger and a holier comprehension of duty.

— *Ella Wheeler Wilcox*

William James, a famous American philosopher and author of Varieties of Religious Experience*, ca. 1895*

Dr. Lewis G. Janes, President of the Brooklyn Ethical Association

To interpret absolute monism worthily, be a mystic. Mystical states of mind in every degree are shown by history, usually though not always, to make for the monistic view. . . . The paragon of all monistic systems is the Vedanta philosophy of Hindostan, and the paragon of Vedantist missionaries was the late Swami Vivekananda who visited our land some years ago. The method of Vedantism is the mystical method. You do not reason, but after going through a certain discipline *you see*, and having seen, you can report the truth. Vivekananda thus reports the truth in one of his lectures here:

"Where is there any more misery for him who sees this Oneness in the universe, this Oneness of life, Oneness of everything?" . . .

I have just been reading some of Vivekananda's addresses in England, which I had not seen. That man is simply a wonder for oratorical power. . . . The swami is an honour to humanity in any case.

— *Professor William James*

At Green Acre [Maine] the swami became a friend of Dr. Lewis G. Janes, Director of the School of Comparative Religions organized by the Green Acre Conference, and President of the Brooklyn Ethical Association. . . .

Dr. Lewis Janes invited the swami to give a series of lectures on the Hindu religion before the Brooklyn Ethical Association. On the evening of 31 December 1894, he gave his first lecture, and according to the report of the Brooklyn Standard, the enthusiastic audience, consisting of doctors and lawyers and judges and teachers, remained spellbound by his eloquent defence of the religion of India. They all acknowledged that Vivekananda was even greater than his fame. At the end of the meeting they made an insistent demand for regular classes in Brooklyn, to which the swami agreed. A series of class meetings was held and several public lectures were given at the Pouch Mansion, where the Ethical Association held its meetings. These lectures constituted the beginning of the permanent work in America which the swami secretly desired.

You write of my dear friend, Vivekananda. I am glad of an opportunity to express my admiration of his character, and it makes me most indignant that anyone should call him in question. He has given us in America higher ideas of life than we have ever had before. In Detroit, an old conservative city, in all the Clubs he is honoured as no one has ever been, and I only feel that all who say one word against him are jealous of his greatness and his fine spiritual perceptions.

He has been a revelation to Christians, . . . he has made possible for us all a diviner and more noble practical life. As a religious teacher and an example to all I do not know of his equal.

Every human being would be made better by knowing him and living in the same house with him. . . . I want everyone in America to know Vivekananda, and if India has more such let her send them to us.

— *Mrs. J. J. Bagley, written to a friend, 22 June 1894*

Mrs. J. J. Bagley, wife of the Governor of Michigan

Sarah J. Farmer, 1897

The community of Green Acre, newly founded by Miss Sarah J. Farmer, was, in a sense, one of the outcomes of the Parliament of Religions. It was a summer colony or retreat on the bank of the Piscataqua River, near Eliot, Maine, the purpose of which was to put into practice the ideal of the harmony of all religions.

There is a mass of thought which is at the present time struggling to get expression. It teaches us that higher direction and not destruction is the law. It teaches us that it is not a world of bad and good, but good and better — and still better. It stops short of nothing but acceptance. . . . It above all teaches that the kingdom of heaven is already in existence if we will have it, that perfection is already in man if he will see it.

The Green Acre meetings last summer were so wonderful, simply because you [Sarah Farmer] opened yourself fully to that thought which has found in you so competent a medium of expression, and because you took your stand on the highest teaching of this thought that the kingdom of heaven already exists.

— *Vivekananda*

Sara Bull, widow of Ole Bull, the celebrated Norwegian violinist. Swamiji used to call her Dhiramata (steady mother).

I am ready to do whatever you advise me to do. You have been a real mother to me. . . . I may have had Divine help — true, but oh, the pound of flesh every bit of Divine help has been to me!! I would be a gladder and better man without that. The present looks very gloomy indeed, but I am a fighter and must die fighting — not give way.

My mistakes have been great, but every one of them was from too much love. How I hate love! Would I had never had any bhakti! Indeed! I wish I could be an Advaitist, calm and heartless. Well, this life is done. I will try in the next.

I went years ago to the Himalayas, never to come back — and my sister committed suicide, the news reached me there, and that weak heart flung me off from the prospect of peace!! It is the weak heart that has driven me out of India to seek some help for those I love, and here I am! Peace have I sought, but the heart, that seat of bhakti, would not allow me to find it. Struggle and torture, torture and struggle! Well, so be it then, since it is my fate; and the quicker it is over, the better.

— *Vivekananda*

Sometimes he [Swamiji] was in a prophetic mood, as on the day when he startled us by saying: "The next great upheaval which is to bring about a new epoch will come from Russia or China. I can't quite see which, but it will be either Russia or China." This he said thirty-two years ago, when China was still under the autocratic rule of the Manchu Emperors, from which there was no prospect of release for centuries to come, and when Czarist Russia was sending the noblest of her people to the Siberian mines. To the ordinary thinker those two countries seemed the most unlikely nations in the world to usher in a new era.

Later he said, "Europe is on the edge of a volcano. Unless the fires are extinguished by a flood of spirituality, it will blow up." This of Europe in 1895, when it was prosperous and at peace. Twenty years later came the explosion!

— *Sister Christine*

Christine Greenstidel, a disciple of Vivekananda

Emma Thursby, a distinguished vocalist, ca. 1900

It was Dora Roethlesberger who took Miss Josephine MacLeod and her sister, Betty, to Vivekananda on 29 January 1895 in New York.

"Years before any of us heard of Swami," Joe related, "Betty, Dora and I were meditating in that room (second floor back in Thirty-fourth Street, New York), just we three, and Dora told us she had seen a man dressed in white whose face she would know anywhere and he broke a beautiful electric blue light over us all. . . . Later, when we knew Swami and he showed us Ramakrishna's picture Dora recognized the man of her vision."

— *Frances Leggett*

Dora Roethlesberger

Emma Thursby took these notes miscellaneously from discourses given by Vivekananda under the "Pine" at Green Acre in July and August 1894:

All souls are playing, some consciously, some unconsciously — Religion is learning to play consciously.

Seek the highest, always the highest, for in the highest is Eternal bliss. If I am to hunt, I will hunt the rhinoceros. If I am to rob, I will rob the treasury of the King. Seek the highest.

Beyond compare, Infinite Oneness — No comparison is possible. Water above, water beneath, water on the right, water on the left; no wave on that water, no ripple, all silence, all eternal bliss. Such will come to thy heart. Seek for nothing else.

Start with the idea that we can finish all experience in this world in this incarnation. We must aim to become perfect in this life this very moment. Success only comes to that life amongst men who wants to do this [this] very moment. . . . Struggle hard and then, if you do not succeed, you are not to blame.

On the twenty-ninth of January 1895, I went with my sister [Betty] to 54 West 33rd Street, New York, and heard the Swami Vivekananda in his sitting room where were assembled fifteen or twenty ladies and two or three gentlemen. The room was crowded. All the arm-chairs were taken; so I sat on the floor in the front row. Swami stood in the corner. He said something, the particular words of which I do not remember, but instantly to me that was truth, and the second sentence he spoke was truth, and the third sentence was truth. And I listened to him for seven years and whatever he uttered was to me truth. From that moment life had a different import. It was as if he made you realize that you were in eternity. It never altered. It never grew. It was like the sun that you will never forget once you have seen. . . .

He used to make us realize there was nothing secular in life; it was all holy. "Always remember, you are incidentally an American, and a woman, but always a child of God. Tell yourself day and night who you are. Never forget it." That is what he used to tell us. His presence, you see, was dynamic. You cannot pass that power on unless you have it, just as you cannot give money away unless you have it. You may imagine it, but you cannot do it.

— *Josephine MacLeod*

Betty Leggett, 1896

Josephine MacLeod, Stuttgart, Germany, 1885 (age 27)

THE LOVE AND ADORATION IN WHICH the swami was held by his Western disciples can hardly be over-emphasized. Some described him as the "lordly monk," and some as a "grand seigneur." . . .

"Mon Prince," Mr. Leggett's courier used to address him. "I am no prince," Swamiji told him, "I am a penniless monk." But the man was not to be put off. "I have travelled with too many princes," he replied; "I know one when I see one!"

He was right, of course; nor was he alone in recognizing nobility when he saw it. "There were but two celebrated personages whom I have met," Mrs. Leggett was to say later, "who could make one feel perfectly at ease without themselves for an instant losing their own dignity — one was the German Emperor, the other, Swami Vivekananda."

Francis H. Leggett, 1896

J. J. Goodwin, an English disciple of Vivekananda

At twenty I was a most unsympathetic, uncompromising fanatic. I would not walk on the foot-path on the theatre side of the street in Calcutta. At thirty-three I can live in the same house with prostitutes and never would think of saying a word of reproach to them. Is it degeneration? Or is it that I am broadening out into that universal love which is the Lord Himself? Again, I have heard that if one does not see the evil round him, he cannot do good work — he lapses into a sort of fatalism. I do not see that. On the contrary, my power of work is immensely increasing and becoming immensely effective. Some days I get into a sort of ecstasy. I feel that I must bless everyone, every being — love and embrace every being — and I literally see that evil is a delusion. I am in one of those moods now, dear Francis, and I am actually shedding tears of joy, as I am writing you now, at the thought of your and Mrs. Leggett's love and kindness to me. I bless the day I was born. I have had so much of kindness and love here, and that Love Infinite who brought me into being has guided every one of my actions, good or bad (don't be frightened); for what am I, what was I ever, but a tool in His hands for whose service I have given up everything — my beloved, my joy, my life, my soul? He is my playful darling. I am His playfellow.

— *Vivekananda*

Mr. Goodwin was the stenographer who had been engaged at 54 West 33rd Street to take down the lectures of Swami Vivekananda. Mr. Goodwin was a court-stenographer, which meant two hundred words a minute, and he was very expensive; but as we did not want to lose any of Vivekananda's words, we engaged him. After the first week Mr. Goodwin refused any money; when they said to him, "What do you mean?" he said, "If Vivekananda gives his life, the least I can do is to give my service." He followed Swami around the world, and we have seven [now eight] volumes hot from his lips that Mr. Goodwin took down. . . .

While we were there [in India, 1898], word came that Mr. Goodwin had died at Ootacamund. When Swamiji learnt that Mr. Goodwin had died, he looked a long long time out upon the snow-capped Himalayas without speaking and presently he said, "My last public utterance is over." And he seldom spoke in public again.

— *Josephine MacLeod*

On 13 February 1896 Vivekananda wrote to E. T. Sturdy of London:

The great electrician Mr. Tesla was charmed to hear about the Vedantic Prana [energy] and Akasha [space] and the Kalpas [cycles], which according to him are the only theories modern science can entertain. Now both Akasha and Prana again are produced from the cosmic Mahat, the Universal Mind, the Brahma or Ishvara. Mr. Tesla thinks he can demonstrate mathematically that force and matter are reducible to potential energy. I am to go and see him next week, to get this new mathematical demonstration.

There is good reason to believe that Mr. Tesla attended Swamiji's lectures in New York in 1896, for about a year later Swamiji remarked during the course of a lecture in South India: "I have myself been told by some of the best scientific minds of the day, how wonderfully rational the conclusions of the Vedanta are. I know one of them personally, who scarcely has time to eat his meal, or go out of his laboratory, but who yet would stand by the hour to attend my lectures on the Vedanta; for, as he expresses it, they are so scientific, they so exactly harmonize with the aspirations of the age and with the conclusions to which modern science is coming at the present time." Swamiji was surely referring here to Nikola Tesla, who did indeed scarcely leave his New York laboratory.

Nikola Tesla (1856-1943), an electrical inventor, ca. 1895

Malvina Hoffman, a famous American sculptor who later made bronze statues of Ramakrishna, Holy Mother, and Vivekananda

One of my vivid memories of childhood [is] an exciting evening spent with a relative of my father's who lived in a modest boarding-house in West Thirty-eighth Street. In the midst of this group of old-fashioned city boarders was introduced suddenly a newcomer — the oriental philosopher and teacher, Swami Vivekananda. When he entered the dining room there was a hush. His dark, bronzed countenance and hands were in sharp contrast to the voluminous, light folds of his turban and robe.

His dark eyes hardly glanced up to notice his neighbours, but there was a sense of tranquillity and power about him that made an imperishable impression upon me. He seemed to personify the mystery and religious "aloofness" of all true teachers of Brahma, and combined with this a kindly and gentle attitude of simplicity towards his fellow men.

— *Malvina Hoffman*

Mme. Emma Calvé, a famous French opera singer

It has been my good fortune and my joy to know a man who truly "walked with God," a noble being, a saint, a philosopher, and a true friend. His influence upon my spiritual life was profound. He opened up new horizons before me; enlarging and vivifying my religious ideas and ideals; teaching me a broader understanding of truth. My soul will bear him eternal gratitude.

This extraordinary man was a Hindu monk of the order of the Vedantas. He was called the Swami Vivekananda, and was widely known in America for his religious teachings. He was lecturing in Chicago one year when I was there; and as I was at that time greatly depressed in mind and body, I decided to go to him, having seen how he had helped some of my friends. . . .

"You must forget," he said as I rose. "Be lively and happy again. Build up your health. Do not dwell in silence upon your sorrows. Transmute your emotions into some form of external expression. Your spiritual health requires it. Your art demands it."

I became once again vivacious and cheerful, thanks to the effect of his powerful will. He did not use any of the ordinary hypnotic or mesmeric influences. It was the strength of his character, the purity and intensity of his purpose, that carried conviction.

— *Emma Calvé*

As there was no hocus-pocus from the beginning, the Vedanta is drawing the attention of the highest classes in American society. Sarah Bernhardt, the French actress, has been playing "Iziel" here [actually Izeyl, in Abbey's Theatre, New York, January, 1896]. It is a sort of Frenchified life of Buddha, where a courtesan "Iziel" wants to seduce the Buddha, under the banyan — and the Buddha preaches to her the vanity of the world, whilst she is sitting all the time in Buddha's lap. However, all is well that ends well — the courtesan fails. Madame Bernhardt acts the courtesan. I went to see the Buddha business — and Madam spying me in the audience wanted to have an interview with me. People here say her voice has the ring of silver strings! Madame Bernhardt has a special regard for India; she tells me again and again that our country is "tres ancien, tres civilise" — very ancient and very civilized.

Sarah Bernhardt, a well-known French actress, as Izeyl

Madame Bernhardt has a very strong desire to visit India. — *"C'est mon rave!* — It is the dream of my life," she says. Again, the Prince of Wales [Edward VII] has promised to take her over to a tiger and elephant hunting excursion. But then she said she must spend some two lakhs of rupees if she went to India! She is of course in no want of money. *"La divine Sarah"* — the divine Sarah — is her name.

— *Vivekananda*

Sister Nivedita, an Irish disciple of Vivekananda

It is strange to remember, and yet it was surely my good fortune, that . . . I heard the teachings of my Master, the Swami Vivekananda, on both the occasions of his visits to England in 1895 and 1896. . . .

This first time we were but fifteen or sixteen guests, intimate friends, many of us, and he sat amongst us, in his crimson robe and girdle, as one bringing us news from a far land, with a curious habit of saying now and again "Shiva! Shiva!" and wearing that look of mingled gentleness and loftiness, that one sees on the faces of those who live much in meditation, that look, perhaps, that Raphael has painted for us, on the brow of the Sistine Child. . . . "What the world wants today is twenty men and women who can dare to stand in the street yonder and say that they possess nothing but God. Who will go?" He had risen to his feet by this time, and stood looking round his audience as if begging some of them to join him. "Why should one fear?" And then, in tones of which, even now, I can hear again the thunderous conviction, "If this is true, what else could matter? *If it is not true, what do our lives matter?*"

— *Sister Nivedita*

Alberta Sturges, (daughter by Betty Leggett's first marriage, and later, Countess of Sandwich), ca. 1896

TO MISS ALBERTA STURGES, ON HER 23RD BIRTHDAY

The mother's heart, the hero's will,
The softest flower's sweetest feel;
The charm and force that ever sway
The altar fire's flaming play;
The strength that leads, in love obeys;
Far-reaching dreams, and patient ways
Eternal faith in Self, in all
The sight Divine in great in small;
All these, and more than I could see
Today may "Mother" grant to thee.

Ever yours with love and blessings,
Vivekananda

Charlotte Elizabeth Sevier

John Henry Sevier

Coming out of one of the swami's lectures [in London], Captain Sevier asked Miss MacLeod, who had already known the swami in America: "You know this young man? Is he what he seems?"

"Yes."

"In that case one must follow him and with him find God."

The Captain went to his wife and said, "Will you let me become the swami's disciple?"

"Yes," she replied.

She asked him, "Will you let me become the swami's disciple?"

He replied with affectionate humour, "I am not so sure!"

The very first time the swami met Mrs. Sevier in private he addressed her as "Mother" and asked her if she would not like to come to India, adding, "I will give you my best realizations."

A very affectionate relationship sprang up between the swami and the Seviers, and the latter regarded him as their son. They became his intimate companions and offered him all their savings. . . .

Through the generosity of the Seviers, the swami, as will be seen, established the Advaita Ashrama at Mayavati in the Himalayas for the training of his disciples, both Eastern and Western, in the contemplation of the Impersonal Godhead. After Captain Sevier's death in the monastery, Mrs. Sevier lived there for fifteen years - the only Western woman in that remote region of the mountains, which is inaccessible for long months of the year - busying herself with the education of the children of the neighbouring hills. Once Miss MacLeod asked her, "Do you not get bored?" "I think of him," she replied, referring to Swami Vivekananda.

Chapel Zur Hohen-Stiege, Saas-Fee, Switzerland, which Swamiji visited in August 1896

Swamiji, Captain and Mrs. Sevier, and Miss Henrietta Müller left Dover on Sunday afternoon, 19 July 1896, for a European tour.

One of those who were with him in the wondrous sojourn at Saas-Fee [in Switzerland] said: "There seemed to be a great light about him and a great stillness and peace. Never have I seen the swami to such advantage. He seemed to communicate spirituality by a look or with a touch. One could almost read his thoughts which were of the highest, so transfigured had his personality become!"

On the way home, there was a little mountain chapel. As the swami saw it, he said quietly, "Do let us offer some flowers at the feet of the Virgin!" His face shone with great tenderness, and he went forth, one of the party accompanying him, and gathered some Alpine flowers. "Offer them at the feet of the Virgin," he said to Mrs. Sevier, "as a token of my gratitude and devotion." And with a strange note of religious certainty, he added, "For She also is the Mother." He would have offered them himself, but feared that his not being a Christian might cause trouble.

It is now some forty years since Vivekananda left this country, but the impression that he left with me is as vivid now as on the day that I said farewell to him.

In fact he had a magnetic personality, associated with great tranquillity. Whether he was walking in the street or standing in a room, there was always the same dignity.

He had a great sense of humour and as a natural correlative, much pathos and pity for affliction. He was a charming companion and entered with ease into any environment he found. And I found that all classes of educated persons that he was brought in contact with looked up to and admired the innate nobility that was in the man. One felt at all times that he was, to use a modern expression, "conscious of the presence of God." In walking, travelling, and leisure times, there constantly came from him some hardly formulated invocation or expression of devotion.

As a teacher he had a great capacity for perceiving the difficulty of an inquirer, and would elucidate it with great simplicity and point to its solution. At the same time he could enter into great intricacies of thought.

— *Edward T. Sturdy*

Edward T. Sturdy, ca. 1902

Professor Max Müller, a famous German Orientalist and author of many books, including Ramakrishna and His Sayings

Max Müller had already published an article on Ramakrishna in the *Nineteenth Century*, entitled "A Real Mahatman." Now he was eager to meet a direct disciple of the Master, and invited Swami Vivekananda to lunch with him in Oxford on 28 May 1896.

The swami was delighted to meet the savant. When the name of Ramakrishna was mentioned, the swami said, "He is worshipped by thousands today, Professor."

"To whom else shall worship be accorded, if not to such?" was Max Müller's reply.

Regarding Max Müller and his wife, the swami later said: "Well, do you know, my impression is that it is Sayana [the commentator of the Vedas] who is born again as Max Müller to revive his own commentary on the Vedas? I have had this notion for long. It became confirmed in my mind, it seems, after I had seen Max Müller. Even here in this country, you don't find a scholar so persevering and so firmly grounded in the Vedas and the Vedanta. Over and above this, what a deep, unfathomable respect for Sri Ramakrishna! Do you know, he believes in his Divine Incarnation! And what great hospitality towards me when I was his guest! Seeing the old man and his lady, it seemed to me that they were living their home-life like another Vasishtha and Arundhati! At the time of parting with me, tears came into the eyes of the old man."

The swami asked Max Müller: "When are you coming to India? All men there would welcome one who has done so much to place the thoughts of their ancestors in a true light."

The face of the aged sage brightened up; there was almost a tear in his eye, a gentle nodding of the head, and slowly the words came out: "I would not return then; you would have to cremate me there."

PROFESSOR DEUSSEN WAS WELL VERSED IN SANSKRIT, and was perhaps the only scholar in Europe who could speak that language fluently. A disciple of Schopenhauer and follower of Kant, Deussen could easily appreciate the high flights of Sankaracharya's

Professor Paul Deussen, a great German Orientalist

philosophy. He believed that the system of Vedanta, as founded on the Upanishads and the *Vedanta Sutras*, is one of the "most majestic structures and valuable products of the genius of man in his search for Truth, and that the highest and purest morality is the immediate consequence of Vedanta."

The swami and the Seviers were cordially received by the German scholar. In the course of the conversation Deussen said that a movement was being made back towards the fountainhead of spirituality, a movement that would in the future probably make India the spiritual leader of the nations, the highest and the greatest spiritual influence on earth. He also found in the swami a vivid demonstration of concentration and control of the mind. On one occasion he saw his guest turning over the pages of a poetical work and did not receive any response to a query. Afterwards the swami apologized, saying that he had been so absorbed in the book that he did not hear the professor. Then he repeated the verses from the book. The conversation soon turned to the power of concentration as developed in the Yoga philosophy. One of the purposes of Deussen's meeting the swami, it is said, was his desire to learn from the latter the secrets of the Yoga powers.

TO PUT THE HINDU IDEAS INTO ENGLISH and then make out of dry philosophy and intricate mythology and queer startling psychology, a religion which shall be easy, simple, popular, and at the same time meet the requirements of the highest minds — is a task only those can understand who have attempted it. The dry, abstract Advaita must become living — poetic — in everyday life; out of hopelessly intricate mythology must come concrete moral forms; and out of bewildering Yogi-ism must come the most scientific and practical psychology — and all this must be put in a form so that a child may grasp it. That is my life's work. . . .

I want to give them [the Westerners] dry, hard reason, softened in the sweetest syrup of love and made spicy with intense work, and cooked in the kitchen of Yoga, so that even a baby can easily digest it.

— *Vivekananda*

London, 1896

At the close of his address [on Sri Ramakrishna, in London, 1896], a white-haired and well-known philosopher said to the swami, "You have spoken splendidly, sir, and I thank you heartily, but you have told us nothing new." The lecturer's sonorous tones rang through the room in reply: "Sir, I have told you the Truth. That, the Truth, is as old as the immemorial hills, as old as humanity, as old as the Creation, as old as the Great God. If I have told it in such words as will make you think, make you live up to your thinking, do I not do well in telling it?" The murmur of "Hear!" "Hear!" and the louder clapping of hands showed how completely the swami had carried his audience with him. . . .

"I will tell you how I came to know the Truth," continued the swami, and in the telling they learned something of the earth-life of Sri Ramakrishna; the sublime simplicity of his character; his indefatigable search for Truth in this religious phase and that; his discovery and his fine proclamation of it: "Where I am, there the Truth is!" . . .

In passages of exquisite eloquence he dilated upon Sri Ramakrishna. Self was utterly forgotten, altogether ignored. . . . "Sri Ramakrishna is the spring of this phase of the earth's religious life, of its impulses and its activities. If I can show the world one glimpse of my Master I shall not live in vain." . . .

"Studying his life I learnt certain things. Of these things that I learnt, two ideas, I think, would be valuable for all humanity. The first [is] the idea of realization — that religion does not consist in erecting temples, or building churches, that it is neither in books, nor words, nor in lectures, nor in societies, it is not in the power of organization, but religion consists in realization. As a fact we all know that nothing will satisfy us until we know the truth for ourselves. However we may argue, however much we may know, but one thing will satisfy us — our own realization. And such an experience is possible for every one of us, if we only try. The first ideal of this attempt to realize religion is that of renunciation; we must give up. As far as we can, we must give up. Darkness and light, enjoyment of the world and enjoyment of God will never go together. Let people try it, if they will. I have seen millions in every country who have tried, but, after all, it comes to nothing. If one word remains true, it is the saying, give up everything for the sake of the Lord. This is a long task, but you can begin it here and now. Bit by bit we must go towards it.

"The second ideal that I have learnt, and which is perhaps the freshest or the newest, is the wonderful truth that the religions of the world are not contradictory nor antagonistic; they are various phases of the one eternal Religion. That Religion is applied to different planes of existence, is applied to the opinions of various minds and various races; there never was my religion or yours, my national religion or your national religion; there never existed many religions; there is only one. The one infinite Religion existed through eternity and will ever exist, and this Religion is expressing itself in various countries in various ways. As such, we must respect them all, and we must try to take them all in as far as we can. Religions manifest themselves not only according to race and geographical position, but according to individual powers. In one it is manifesting itself as intense activity, as work. In another it is manifesting itself as mysticism, in another it is manifesting itself in philosophy, and so forth. It is wrong when we say to others your methods are not right. . . . To learn this one central secret, that the Truth may be one and yet many at the same time, that we may have different visions of the same Truth from different standpoints, is exactly what has got to be. . . . And this idea, above all other ideas, I find to be the crying need of the day." ❧

London, December 1896

VII

"Arise! Awake! And Stop not Till the Goal is Reached!"

After staying three and a half years in the West, Vivekananda returned to India with some of his Western disciples. He arrived at Colombo on 15 January 1897 and received a triumphal reception. When he reached south India, millions of people paid homage to the swami, and even the rajas prostrated themselves before him. He travelled all over India, this time as a national hero. He began to awaken the sleeping, subjugated nation with the clarion call of Vedanta:

"Arise! Awake! And stop not till the goal is reached!" "Strength, strength is what the Upanishads speak to me from every page. Be not weak. Will sin cure sin, weakness cure weakness? Stand up and be strong." "The first step in getting strength is to uphold the Upanishads, and believe: 'I am the Soul. I am the Omnipotent, I am the Omniscient.' Repeat these blessed saving words. . . . These conceptions of Vedanta must come out, must not remain only in the forest, not only in the cave, but they must come out at the bar and the bench, in the pulpit, and in the cottage of the poor man."

Vivekananda knew the pros and cons of organized religion. While he was in America he had this thought: "To organize or not to organize? If I organize, the spirit will diminish. If I do not organize, the message will not spread." Therefore, on 1 May 1897 Swamiji founded the Ramakrishna Mission in Calcutta and framed its rules and regulations. He delineated the aims and ideals of the Ramakrishna Order, which is purely spiritual and humanitarian in nature and is completely dissociated from politics. He started two centres — one at Mayavati in the Himalayas, where Westerners could practise nondualistic Vedanta, and the other in Madras. He also started three magazines — *Brahmavadin* (now defunct), *Prabuddha Bharata*, and *Udbodhan* — to propagate the ideas and ideals of Vedanta and Sri Ramakrishna.

Meanwhile Vivekananda was receiving heartwarming letters from his Western disciples and friends about the Vedanta work. One letter was signed by Lewis G. Janes, President of the Brooklyn Ethical Association; C. C. Everett, Dean of the Harvard Divinity School; William James and Josiah Royce, both professors of philosophy at Harvard University; Mrs. Sara C. Bull (also known as Mrs. Ole Bull), the promoter of the Cambridge Conferences; and others. It runs: "As members of the Cambridge Conferences, devoted to comparative study in Ethics, Philosophy, and Religion, it gives us great pleasure to recognize the value of your able expositions of the Philosophy and Religion of Vedanta in America and the interest created thereby among thinking people." The swami's Detroit friends wrote: "We, Western Aryans, have been so long separated from our Eastern brothers that we had almost forgotten our identity of origin, until you came and, with beautiful presence and matchless eloquence, rekindled within our hearts the knowledge that we of America and you of India are one."

In 1898 a piece of property was purchased at Belur, across the river from Calcutta, which became the headquarters of the Ramakrishna Order. Swamiji began to train his brother monks and disciples so that they could properly carry on the work. But his health began to fail as a result of constant work. He badly needed rest. His American disciples and friends wanted him to return to America, and his brother disciples also felt that a sea voyage would do him good.

Colombo, January 1897

O India! Forget not that the ideal of thy womanhood is Sita, Savitri, Damayanti; forget not that the God thou worshippest is the great Ascetic of ascetics, the all-renouncing Shankara, the Lord of Uma; forget not that thy marriage, thy wealth, thy life are not for sense pleasure, are not for thy individual personal happiness; forget not that thou art born as a sacrifice to the Mother's altar; forget not that thy social order is but the reflex of the Infinite Universal Motherhood; forget not that the lower classes, the ignorant, the poor, the illiterate, the cobbler, the sweeper, are thy flesh and blood, thy brothers. Thou brave one, be bold, take courage, be proud that thou art an Indian, and proudly proclaim, "I am an Indian, every Indian is my brother." Say, "The ignorant Indian, the poor and destitute Indian, the Brahmin Indian, the Pariah Indian, is my brother."

Faith, faith, faith in ourselves, faith, faith in God — this is the secret of greatness. If you have faith in all the three hundred and thirty millions of your mythological gods, and in all the gods which foreigners have now and again introduced into your midst, and still have no faith in yourselves, there is no salvation for you. Have faith in yourselves, and stand up on that faith and be strong; that is what we need. Why is it that we three hundred and thirty millions of people have been ruled for the last one thousand years by any and every handful of foreigners who chose to walk over our prostrate bodies? Because they had faith in themselves and we had not. I saw that inside the national hearts of both Europe and America resides the tremendous power of the men's faith in themselves. An English boy will tell you, "I am an Englishman, and I can do anything." The American boy will tell you the same thing, and so will any European boy. Can our boys say the same thing here? No, nor even the boys' fathers. We have lost faith in ourselves. Therefore to preach the Advaita [nondual] aspect of the Vedanta is necessary to rouse up the hearts of men, to show them the glory of their souls.

— *Vivekananda*

Colombo, January 1897

Colombo, January 1897

Shiva Temple at Rameshwaram

My India, arise! Where is your vital force? In your Immortal Soul. Each nation, like each individual, has one theme in this life, which is its centre, the principal note round which every other note comes to form the harmony. If any one nation attempts to throw off its national vitality, the direction which has become its own through the transmission of centuries, that nation dies. . . . In one nation political power is its vitality, as in England. Artistic life, in another, and so on. In India religious life forms the centre, the keynote of the whole music of the national life. And therefore, if you succeed in the attempt to throw off your religion and take up either politics or society, the result will be that you will become extinct. Social reform and politics have to be preached through the vitality of your religion. . . . Every man has to make his own choice; so has every nation. We made our choice ages ago. And it is the faith in an Immortal Soul. I challenge anyone to give it up. How can you change your nature?

❧ ❧ ❧

He who sees Shiva in the poor, in the weak, and in the diseased, really worships Shiva; and if he sees Shiva only in the image, his worship is but preliminary.

A rich man had a garden and two gardeners. One of these gardeners was very lazy and did not work; but when the owner came to the garden, the lazy man would get up and fold his arms and say, "How beautiful is the face of my master," and dance before him. The other gardener would not talk much, but would work hard, and produce all sorts of fruits and vegetables which he would carry on his head to his master who lived a long way off. Of these two gardeners, which would be the more beloved of his master? Shiva is that master, and this world is His garden, and there are two sorts of gardeners here: the one who is lazy, hypocritical, and does nothing, only talking about Shiva's beautiful eyes and nose and other features; and the other, who is taking care of Shiva's children, all those that are poor and weak, all animals, and all His creation. Which of these would be the more beloved of Shiva? Certainly he that serves His children. It is said in the Shastra [scripture] that those who serve the servants of God are His greatest servants. So you will bear this in mind.

— *Vivekananda*

Madras, February 1897

Feel, therefore, my would-be reformers, my would-be patriots! Do you feel? Do you feel that millions and millions of the descendants of gods and of sages have become next-door neighbours to brutes? Do you feel that millions are starving today and millions have been starving for ages? Do you feel that ignorance has come over the land as a dark cloud? Does it make you restless? Does it make you sleepless? Has it made you almost mad? Are you seized with that one idea of the misery of ruin, and have you forgotten all about your name, your fame, your wives, your children, your property, even your own bodies? If so, that is the first step to becoming a patriot. For centuries people have been taught theories of degradation. They have been told that they are nothing. The masses have been told all over the world that they are not human beings. They have been so frightened for centuries that they have nearly become animals. Never were they allowed to hear of the Atman. Let them hear of the Atman — that even the lowest of the low have the Atman within, who never dies and never is born — Him whom the sword cannot pierce, nor the fire burn, nor the air dry, immortal, without beginning or end, the all-pure, omnipotent, and omnipresent Atman.

I was asked by a young lady in London, "What have you Hindus done? You have never even conquered a single nation." That is true from the point of view of the Englishman, but from ours it is quite the opposite. . . .

Our message has gone out to the world many a time, but slowly, silently, unperceived. It is on a par with everything in India. The one characteristic of Indian thought is its silence, its calmness.

To my mind that is the argument why our religion is truer than any other religion, because it never conquered, because it never shed blood, because its mouth always shed on all, words of blessing, of peace, words of love and sympathy. It is here and here alone that the ideals of toleration were first preached. And it is here and here alone that toleration and sympathy have become practical; it is theoretical in every other country; it is here and here alone, that the Hindu builds mosques for the Mohammendans and churches for the Christians.

Like the gentle dew that falls unseen and unheard, and yet brings into blossom the fairest of roses, has been the contribution of India to the thought of the world. Silent, unperceived, yet omnipotent in its effect, it has revolutionized the thought of the world, yet nobody knows when it did so.

— *Vivekananda*

Madras, February 1897

Castle Kernan, where Vivekananda stayed in Madras. It has now been renamed "Vivekananda House."

I may also here say that from the first day on which he reached the Castle Kernan, and up to the last, his residence was at all times crowded with visitors from all classes of the population and by the people of both sexes. Many delicate and retiring women of high and respectable families approached the Castle Kernan as if they were visiting a temple. . . .

— *K. Sundararama Iyer*

He said to me and my father, "Practical patriotism means not a mere sentiment or even emotion of love of the motherland but a passion to serve our fellow-countrymen. I have gone all over India on foot and have seen with my own eyes the ignorance, misery, and squalor of our people. My whole soul is afire and I am burning with a fierce desire to change such evil conditions. Let no one talk of karma. If it was their karma to suffer; it is our karma to relieve the suffering. If you want to find God, serve Man. To reach Narayana [God] you must serve the daridra-narayanas — the starving millions of India." That was the root from which came the great tree of the Ramakrishna Mission later on. His words melted our hearts and kindled in our souls the flame of social service. Thus service was as dear to him as spirituality.

— *K. S. Ramaswami Sastri (K. S. Iyer's son)*

On reaching Madras, however, in 1897, Vivekananda boldly claimed that even the utmost realizations of Dualism [of Madhva] and Qualified Nondualism [of Ramanuja], were but stages on the way to Nondualism [of Shankara] itself; and the final bliss, for all alike, was the mergence in One without a second. It is said that at one of his midday question classes, a member of his audience asked him why, if this was the truth, it had never before been mentioned by any of the Masters. It was customary to give answers to these questions, first in English and then in Sanskrit, for the benefit of such scholars present as knew no modern language, and the great gathering was startled, on this occasion, to hear the reply, "Because I was born for this, and it was left for me to do!"

— *Sister Nivedita*

Madras, February 1897
Standing, left to right: *A few children, Alasinga Perumal, J. J. Goodwin, M. N. Banerjee, and other local devotees.* Sitting on chairs, left to right: *Tarapada (an outside Sadhu), Swamis Shivananda, Vivekananda, Niranjanananda and Sadananda.* Front row: *(second) Biligiri Iyengar, (fourth) M. C. Nanjunda Rao*

Reception in Calcutta, 28 February 1897

Calcutta, February 1897

Friend, let me speak my heart to thee.
One lesson I have learnt in life:
This dreadful world is tossed with waves,
And one boat only fares across.
Study of scripture, sacred words,
Restraint of breath, conflicting schools,
Dispassion, science, philosophy,
Sense pleasure, are but freaks of mind.
Love! Love! — that is the only jewel!
In soul and Brahman, man and God,
In ghosts and spirits without shape,
In angels, beasts, birds, insects, worms,
Dwells Love, deep in the hearts of all. . . .

From highest Brahman to the worm,
Even to the atom's inmost core,
All things with Love are interfused.
Friend, offer body, mind, and soul
In constant service at their feet.
Thy God is here before thee now,
Revealed in all these myriad forms:
Rejecting them, where seekest thou
His presence? He who freely shares
His love with every living thing
Proffers true service unto God.

— *Vivekananda* (To a Friend, *a poem*)

On 28 February 1897, he [Swamiji] was given a public reception in Calcutta. Raja Benoy Krishna Deb presided, and five thousand people jammed the meeting. As usual, the swami asked the people to go back to the perennial philosophy of the Upanishads. He also paid a touching tribute to Ramakrishna, "my teacher, my master, my hero, my ideal, my God in life." "If there has been anything achieved by me," he said with deep feeling, "by thoughts or words or deeds, if from my lips has ever fallen one word that has ever helped anyone in the world, I lay no claim to it; it was his. But if there have been curses falling from my lips, if there has been hatred coming out of me, it is all mine, and not his. All that has been weak has been mine; all that has been life-giving, strengthening, pure, and holy has been his inspiration, his words, and he himself. Yes, my friends, the world has yet to know that man." A few days later, he gave another public lecture at the Star Theatre, Calcutta, on "Vedanta in All Its Phases."

Calcutta, February 1897

Gopal Lal Seal's garden house, Cossipore, March 1897
Standing, left to right: *Shantiram Babu, Mr. Turnbull, Swami Prakashananda, Singaravelu Mudaliar (Kidi), Swami Vivekananda, Captain Sevier, Swami Shivananda, unidentified person.* Sitting, left to right: *Alasinga Perumal, Swami Ramakrishnananda, Swami Premananda, Mrs. Sevier, Swami Adbhutananda, Swami Turiyananda, G. G. Narasimhachariar.* Floor, left to right: *Unidentified person, Mr. Harrison of Colombo*

One day a young man complained to the swami that he could not make progress in spiritual life. He had worshipped images, following the advice of one teacher, and had tried to make his mind void according to the instruction of another, but all had been fruitless.

"Sir," the young man said, "I sit still in meditation, shutting the door of my room, and keep my eyes closed as long as I can, but I do not find peace of mind. Can you show me the way?"

"My boy," replied the swami in a voice full of loving sympathy, "if you take my word, you will have first of all to open the door of your room and look around, instead of closing your eyes. There are hundreds of poor and helpless people in your neighbourhood; you have to serve them to the best of your ability. You will have to nurse and procure food and medicine for the sick. You will have to feed those who have nothing to eat. You will have to teach the ignorant. My advice to you is that if you want peace of mind, you shall have to serve others to the best of your ability."

Swamiji: Within there is the lion — the eternally pure, illumined, and ever-free Atman; and directly one realizes Him through meditation and concentration, this world of maya vanishes.

Disciple: Sir, I have only read of these things in the scriptures, but nothing has been realized as yet.

Swamiji: It is bound to come in time. But some attain this early, and others are a little late. One must stick to it — determined never to let it go. This is true manliness. . . .

Sometimes the mind is concentrated on a set of ideas — this is called meditation with vikalpa, or oscillation. But when the mind becomes almost free from all activities, it melts in the inner Self, which is the essence of infinite Knowledge, One, and Itself Its own support. This is what is called nirvikalpa samadhi, free from all activities. In Sri Ramakrishna we have again and again noticed both these forms of samadhi. He had not to struggle to get these states. They came to him spontaneously, then and there. It was a wonderful phenomenon. It was by seeing him that we could rightly understand these things. Meditate every day alone. Everything will open up of itself.

At 8 Bosepara Lane, Calcutta, 20 June (?) 1899
Left to right: *Swamis Trigunatitananda, Shivananda, Vivekananda, Turiyananda, and Brahmananda.* Below: *Swami Sadananda*

On 1 May 1897 Swami Vivekananda called a meeting of the monastic and lay devotees of Sri Ramakrishna at the house of the Master's intimate disciple Balaram Bose, for the purpose of establishing his work on an organized basis. . . .

Swami Vivekananda proposed to the members present that the Association should "Bear the name of him in whose name we have become sannyasins, taking whom as your ideal you are leading the life of householders, and whose holy name, influence, and teachings have, within twelve years of his passing away, spread in such an unthought-of-way both in the East and in the West." All the members enthusiastically approved of the swami's proposal, and the Ramakrishna Mission Association came into existence.

The aim of the Association was to spread the truths that Ramakrishna, for the good of humanity, had preached and taught through the example of his own life, and to help others to put them into practice for their physical, mental, and spiritual advancement.

Ay, a glorious destiny, my brethren, for as far back as the days of the Upanishads we have thrown the challenge to the world: "Not by progeny, not by wealth, but by renunciation alone immortality is reached." Race after race has taken the challenge up and tried their utmost to solve the world-riddle on the plane of desires. They have all failed in the past — the old ones have become extinct under the weight of wickedness and misery, which lust for power and gold brings in its train, and the new ones are tottering to their fall. The question has yet to be decided whether peace will survive or war; whether patience will survive or non-forbearance; whether goodness will survive or wickedness; whether muscle will survive or brain; whether worldliness will survive or spirituality. We have solved our problem ages ago, and held on to it through good or evil fortune, and mean to hold on to it till the end of time. Our solution is unworldliness — renunciation.

— *Vivekananda*

Balaram Bose's house in Calcutta

Kashmir, 1898

Kashmir, 1898

As for myself I am quite content. I have roused a good many of our people, and that was all I wanted. Let things have their course and karma its sway. I have no bonds here below. I have seen life, and it is all self — life is for self, love for self, honour for self, everything for self. I look back and scarcely find any action I have done for self — even my wicked deeds were not for self. So I am content; not that I feel I have done anything specially good or great, but the world is so little, life so mean a thing, existence so, so servile — that I wonder and smile that human beings, rational souls, should be running after this self — so mean and detestable a prize.

This is the truth. We are caught in a trap, and the sooner one gets out, the better for one. I have seen the truth — let the body float up or down, who cares?

IT WOULD HAVE MADE YOUR HEART glad to see how my boys are working in the midst of famine and disease and misery — nursing by the mat-bed of the cholera stricken pariah and feeding the starving chandala, and the Lord sends help to me, to them, to all. He is with me, the Beloved, as He was when I was in America, in England, when I was roaming about unknown from place to place in India. . . .

I feel my task is done — at most three or four years more of life are left. I have lost all wish for my salvation. I never wanted earthly enjoyments. I must see my machine in strong working order, and then, knowing for sure that I have put in a lever for the good of humanity, in India at least, which no power can drive back, I will sleep — without caring what will be next.

And may I be born again and again, and suffer thousands of miseries, so that I may worship the only God that exists, the only God I believe in, the sum total of all souls. And above all, my God the wicked, my God the miserable, my God the poor of all races, of all species, is the especial object of my worship.

— *Vivekananda*

My whole ambition in life is to set in motion a machinery which will bring noble ideas to the door of everybody, and then let men and women settle their own fate. Let them know what our forefathers as well as other nations have thought on the most momentous questions of life. Let them see specially what others are doing now, and then decide. We are to put the chemicals together, the crystallization will be done by nature according to her laws. Work hard, be steady, and have faith in the Lord. Set to work, I am coming sooner or later. Keep the motto before you — "Elevation of the masses without injuring their religion." . . . Have faith in yourselves, great convictions are the mothers of great deeds. Onward forever! Sympathy for the poor, the downtrodden, even unto death — this is our motto.

Religion for a long time has come to be static in India. What we want is to make it dynamic. I want it to be brought into the life of everybody. Religion, as it always has been in the past, must enter the palaces of kings as well as the homes of the poorest peasants in the land. Religion, the common inheritance, the universal birthright of the race, must be brought free to the door of everybody.

— *Vivekananda*

Sharat Chandra Chakrabarty, a disciple of Vivekananda

Kashmir, 1897. Sitting on chairs, left to right: *Swamis Sadananda, Vivekananda, Niranjanananda, and Dhirananda*

Disciple (*Sharat Chandra Chakrabarty*): Sir, what is the necessity for doing good to others?

Swamiji: Well, it is necessary for one's own good. We become forgetful of the ego when we think of the body as dedicated to the service of others — the body, which most complacently we identify with the ego. And in the long run comes the loss of body-consciousness. The more intently you think of the well-being of others, the more oblivious of yourself you become. In this way, as your heart gradually gets purified by work, you will come to feel the truth that your own Self is pervading all beings and all things. Thus it is that doing good to others constitutes a way, a means, of revealing one's own Self, or Atman. Know this also to be one of the spiritual practices, a discipline for God-realization. Its aim also is Self-realization. Exactly as that aim is attained by jnana [knowledge], bhakti [devotion], and so on, so also by work for the sake of others.

Kashmir, 1898. Left to right: *Josephine MacLeod, Mrs. Ole Bull, Vivekananda, and Sister Nivedita*

On a house boat in Kashmir, 1898. Left to right: *Josephine MacLeod, Vivekananda, Mrs. Ole Bull, and Sister Nivedita*

In Kashmir [in the summer of 1898] the swami pined for solitude. The desire for the solitary life of a monk became irresistible; and he would often break away from the little party to roam alone. After his return he would make some such remark as: "It is a sin to think of the body," "It is wrong to manifest power," or "Things do not grow better; they remain as they are. It is we who grow better, by the changes we make in ourselves." Often he seemed to be drifting without any plan, and the disciples noticed his strange detachment. "At no time," Sister Nivedita wrote, "would it have surprised us had someone told us that today or tomorrow he would be gone forever, that we were listening to his voice for the last time."

This planlessness was observed in him more and more as his earthly existence drew towards its end. Two years later, when Sister Nivedita gave him a bit of worldly advice, the swami exclaimed in indignation: "Plans! Plans! That is why you Western people can never create a religion! If any of you ever did, it was only a few Catholic saints who had no plans. Religion was never, never preached by planners!"

Ready for fun as the swami usually was, he postponed a contemplated journey to organize for his American friends a surprise celebration of the Fourth of July, their national festival. Taking the one non-American member of the party into his confidence, he went out late on the afternoon of 3 July and in great excitement brought back a brahmin tailor. He asked his English disciple to explain to the man how to make a replica of the American flag. The stars and stripes were crudely represented on a piece of cotton cloth. This was nailed to the head of the dining-room boat, where an early tea was arranged, and surrounded with branches of the evergreens. As his own special contribution to the occasion, he wrote a poem that was read aloud by way of greeting. It was entitled "To the Fourth of July," and can be interpreted as a passionate utterance of his own longing for the Final Freedom in the Infinite. Time was to prove that it had been penned in a prophetic vein; for, four years later, on that very day, his shackles of work broken, he entered in "Springing joy" into the Final Freedom, concerning which he had written.

Kashmir, 1898

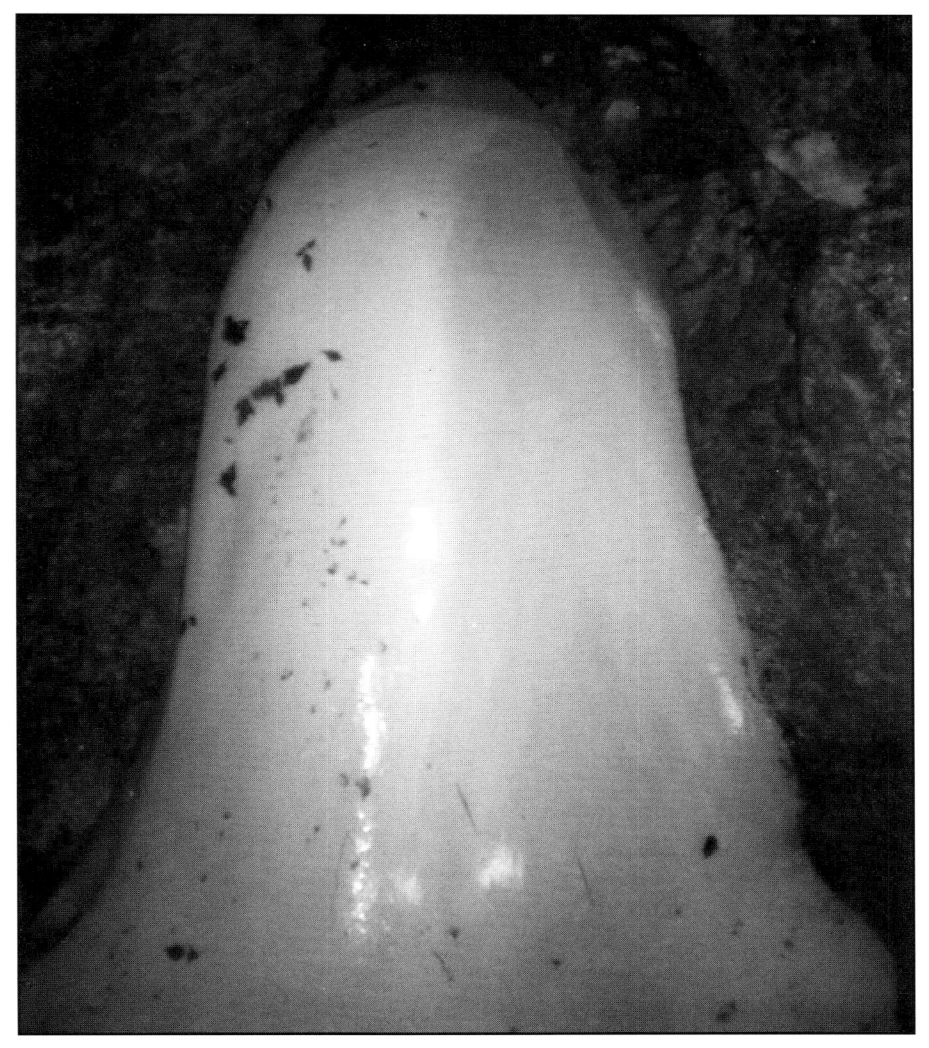

Ice-linga, Amarnath Cave, Kashmir

Once [20 July 1898] in Kashmir, after an attack of illness I had seen him [Swamiji] lift a couple of pebbles, saying "Whenever death approaches me, all weakness vanishes. I have neither fear, nor doubt, nor thought of the external. I simply busy myself making ready to die. I am as hard as *that*" — and the stones struck one another in his hand — "for I *have* touched the feet of God!"

On Tuesday, August the 2nd [1898], the great day of Amarnath, the first batch of pilgrims must have left the camp at two! We left by the light of the full moon. The sun rose as we went down the narrow valley. . . .

Half an hour later he [Swamiji] entered the cave. With a smile he knelt, first at one end of the semicircle, then at the other. The place was vast, large enough to hold a cathedral, and the great ice-Shiva, in a niche of deepest shadow, seemed as if throned on its own base. A few minutes passed, and then he turned to leave the cave.

To him, the heavens had opened. He had touched the feet of Shiva. He had had to hold himself tight, he said afterwards, lest he "should swoon away." . . .

Afterwards he would often tell of the overwhelming vision that had seemed to draw him almost into its vertex. He would talk of the poetry of the white ice-pillar, and it was he who suggested that the first discovery of the place had been by a party of shepherds, who had wandered far in search of their flocks one summer day, and had entered the cave to find themselves, before the unmelting ice, in the presence of the Lord Himself. He always said too that the grace of Amarnath had been granted to him there, not to die till he himself should give consent.

— *Sister Nivedita*

Kshirbhavani Temple, Kashmir

Calcutta, February 1897

On 30 September 1898 Swami Vivekananda retired to a temple of the Divine Mother, where he stayed alone for a week. There he worshipped the Deity, known as Kshirbhavani, following the time-honoured ritual, praying and meditating like a humble pilgrim.

He had a vision of the Goddess and found Her a living Deity. But the temple had been destroyed by the Muslim invaders, and the image placed in a niche surrounded by ruins. Surveying this desecration, the swami felt distressed at heart and said to himself: "How could the people have permitted such sacrilege without offering strenuous resistance? If I had been here then, I would never have allowed such a thing. I would have laid down my life to protect the Mother." Thereupon he heard the voice of the Goddess saying: "What if unbelievers should enter My temple and defile My image? What is that to you? Do *you* protect Me, or do *I* protect you? . . . If I so wish I can have innumerable temples and monastic centres. I can even this moment raise a seven-storied golden temple on this very spot." . . . Referring to this experience after his return, he said to his disciples: "All my patriotism is gone. Everything is gone. Now it is only 'Mother! Mother!'"

In October 1898 Sharat Chandra Chakrabarty wrote:

It is two or three days since Swamiji has returned from Kashmir. His health is indifferent. When the disciple came to Belur Math, Swami Brahmananda said, "Since returning from Kashmir, Swamiji does not speak to anybody, he sits in one place rapt in thought; you go to him and by conversation try to draw his mind a little towards worldly objects."

The disciple coming to Swamiji's room in the upper storey found him sitting as if immersed in deep meditation. There was no smile on his face, his brilliant eyes had no outward look, as if intent on seeing something within.

When even after a long time Swamiji did not speak, the disciple was a little troubled at heart and touching his feet said, "Won't you relate to me what things you have seen at Amarnath?" By the disciple's touching his feet, the tensity of his mood was broken a little, as if his attention was diverted a little outwards. He said, "Since visiting Amarnath, I feel as if Shiva is sitting on my head for twenty-four hours and will not come down." The disciple heard it with speechless wonder.

Swamiji [further] said, "Since hearing that Divine Voice [in Kshirbhavani] I cherish no more plans. The idea of building Maths etc. I have given up; as Mother wills, so it will be."

In a day or two we went up to see Swami at his temporary monastery at Belur, at Nilambar Mukherjee's garden house. During the afternoon Swami said, "I must take you to the new monastery that we are buying." I said, "O, but Swami, isn't this big enough?" It was a lovely little villa he had, with perhaps an acre or two of land, a small lake and many flowers. I thought it was big enough for anyone. But he evidently saw things in a different scale. So he took us across little gullies to the place where is now the present monastery. Mrs. Ole Bull and I, finding this old riverside house empty, said, "Swami, can't we use this house?" "It isn't in order," he answered. "But we'll put it in order," we told him. With that he gave us permission. So we had it all newly whitewashed and went down to the bazars, bought old mahogany furniture and made a drawing-room, half of which was Indian style and half of which was Western style. We had an outside dining room, our bedroom, and an extra room for Sister Nivedita, who was our guest until we went to Kashmir. We stayed there quite two months. It was perhaps the most beautiful time we ever had with Swamiji. He came every morning for early tea which he used to take under the great mango tree. That tree is still in existence. We never allowed them to cut it down, though they were keen to do it. He loved our living at that riverside cottage; and he would bring all those who came to visit him, to see what a charming home we had made of this house he had thought uninhabitable. In the afternoons we used to give tea parties in front of the house, in full view of the river, where always could be seen loads of boats going upstream, we receiving as if we were in our own drawing-rooms. Swamiji loved all that intimate use we made of things which they took as a matter of course. One night there came one of those deluges of rain, like sheets of water. He paced up and down our outside dining room veranda, talking of Krishna and the love of Krishna and the power that love was in the world. He had a curious quality that when he was a *bhakta*, a lover, he brushed aside *karma* and *raja* and *jnana yogas* as if they were of no consequence whatever. And when he was a *karma-yogi*, then he made that the great theme. Or equally so, the *jnana*. Sometimes, weeks, he would fall in one particular mood utterly disregardful of what he had been, just previous to that. He seemed to be filled with an amazing power of concentration; of opening up to the great Cosmic qualities that are all about us. It was probably that power of concentration that kept him so young and so fresh. He never seemed to repeat himself. There would be an incident of very little consequence which would illuminate a whole new passage for him. And he had such a place for us Westerners whom he called "Living Vedantins." He would say: "When you believe a thing is true, you do it, you do not dream about it. That is your power."

— *Josephine MacLeod*

Belur Math during Vivekananda's time

Nilambar Babu's garden house (now part of Belur Math)

Old shrine at Belur Math as it was during Vivekananda's time

On 9 December 1898 the Ramakrishna Monastery at Belur was formally consecrated by the swami. . . . The swami himself had performed the worship on that occasion and afterwards had carried on his shoulder the copper vessel containing the Master's sacred relics. While bearing it he had said to a disciple: "The Master once told me, 'I will go and live wherever you take me, carrying me on your shoulder, be it under a tree or in the humblest cottage.' With faith in that gracious promise I myself am now carrying him to the site of our future Math. Know for certain, my boy, that so long as his name inspires his followers with the ideal of purity, holiness, and charity for all men, even so long shall he, the Master, sanctify this place with his presence."

Of the glorious future he saw for the monastery the swami said: "It will be a centre in which will be recognized and practised a grand harmony of all creeds and faiths as exemplified in the life of Sri Ramakrishna, and religion in its universal aspect, alone, will be preached. And from this centre of universal toleration will go forth the shining message of good will, peace, and harmony to deluge the whole world." He warned all of the danger of sectarianism's creeping in if they became careless.

A parting address was given to Swamiji by the junior sannyasins of the (Belur) Math, on the eve of his leaving for the West for the second time. The following is the substance of Swamiji's reply as entered in the Math diary on 19 June 1899:

This is not the time for a long lecture. But I shall speak to you in brief about a few things which I should like you to carry into practice. First, we have to understand the ideal, and then the methods by which we can make it practical. Those of you who are sannyasins must try to do good to others, for sannyasa means that. . . .

One must learn sooner or later that one cannot get salvation if one does not try to seek the salvation of his brothers. You must try to combine in your life immense idealism with immense practicality. You must be prepared to go into deep meditation now, and the next moment you must be ready to go and cultivate these fields [Swamiji said, pointing to the meadows of the Math]. You must be prepared to explain the difficult intricacies of the scriptures now, and the next moment to go and sell the produce of the fields in the market. You must be prepared for all menial services, not only here, but elsewhere also. ❧

Belur Math, 19 June 1899
Standing, left to right: *Devendra Mazumdar, Swamis Nirmalananda, Virajananda, Shivananda, Turiyananda, Akhandananda, Vijnanananda, Saradananda, Satchidananda, Mahendra Nath Datta, and U. N. Dev.* Sitting on chair, left to right: *Swami Vivekananda and Nadu (Brahmachari Harendranath).* Sitting on bench, left to right: *Br. Krishnalal, Swamis Somananda, Kalyanananda, Advaitananda, Atmananda, Sadananda, Sureshwarananda, and Bodhananda, Br. Nandalal, Khanda, Swami Prakashananda, Br. Brajen, and Swami Shuddhananda.* Below: *Swami Nishchayananda*

VIII

East Meets West – II

On 20 June 1899 Vivekananda left for the West for the second time accompanied by Swami Turiyananda and Sister Nivedita. This journey with the swami turned into a wonderful education for both of them. He trained Turiyananda in how to work in the West and Nivedita in how to work in the East. One day, before leaving India he had said to Nivedita: "Social life in the West is like a peal of laughter, but underneath, it is a wail. It ends in a sob. The fun and frivolity are all on the surface: really, it is full of tragic intensity. Now here [India], it is sad and gloomy on the outside, but underneath are carelessness and merriment."

Vivekananda's belief in the effectiveness of Vedanta grew through his travels and observations, experiences and insights. He saw it not as a mere religion or philosophy, but rather as a means to reconcile science and religion, and to harmonize material prosperity and spirituality. He noticed that the East was strong in noble religious and spiritual traditions even though it suffered from grinding poverty; and that the West, for all its technological advancements and affluence, suffered from spiritual poverty. There was no reason, he thought, why East and West could not profit from each other's strengths by removing each other's weaknesses.

Vivekananda arrived in London on 31 July 1899 and stayed a couple of weeks. He met with some of his old friends, but did not lecture because of his fragile health. He then left for New York with Turiyananda and two American devotees, arriving there on 28 August. It was arranged that the swamis should live temporarily at Ridgely, the beautiful country home of Mr. Francis Leggett. That fall Vivekananda rested and gradually recuperated. He was happy seeing the activities of the Vedanta Society of New York (which he had founded in November 1894) under the leadership of Swami Abhedananda; and he engaged Turiyananda to give classes in Montclair, New Jersey.

On 22 November the swami left for Los Angeles via Chicago. Vivekananda stayed in southern California from 3 December 1899 to 22 February 1900 and gave several lectures in Los Angeles and Pasadena. He then went to northern California and founded the Vedanta Society of San Francisco. Swamiji's oratory and magnetic personality overwhelmed the people. "He once told us," Mr. Thomas Allan recounted, "that he had such faith in the Divine Mother that if he had to speak on a subject that he knew absolutely nothing about, he would get on his feet, for he knew that Mother would put the words into his mouth."

During his second visit, Swamiji worked mainly in California. He had a premonition of his approaching end and wrote to Miss MacLeod, "My boat is nearing the calm harbour from which it is never more to be driven out."

Swamiji left California on 30 May and reached New York via Chicago on 7 June. He sent Turiyananda to start a retreat in northern California, which later became Shanti Ashrama. Swamiji gave a few more lectures and classes in New York and then left for Paris on 26 July to attend the Congress of the History of Religions. He spoke twice there and closed his Western mission. He then visited some countries in Europe with Madame Emma Calvé and Miss Josephine MacLeod, finally returning to India in December 1900.

Swami Vivekananda announced his plan to go to the West to inspect the work he had founded and to fan the flame. The devotees and friends welcomed the idea since they thought the sea voyage would restore his failing health. He planned to take with him Sister Nivedita and Swami Turiyananda.

Versed in the scriptures, Turiyananda had spent most of his life in meditation and was averse to public work. Failing to persuade him by words to accompany him to America, Vivekananda put his arms round his brother disciple's neck and wept like a child, saying: "Dear brother, don't you see how I am laying down my life inch by inch in fulfilling the mission of my Master? Now I have come to the verge of death! Can you look on without trying to relieve part of my great burden?"

Swami Turiyananda was deeply moved and offered to follow the swami wherever he wanted to go. When he asked if he should take with him some Vedanta scriptures, Vivekananda said: "Oh, they have had enough of learning and books! The last time they saw a warrior [referring to himself, who had delivered his message in a combative spirit]; now I want to show them a brahmin."

Swami Turiyananda, San Francisco, ca. 1900

A group photo in Belur Math, 19 June 1899

THE STEAMSHIP *GOLCONDA*, CARRYING the swami and his two companions, touched Madras, but the passengers were not allowed to land on account of the plague in Calcutta. This was a great disappointment to Swami Vivekananda's South Indian friends. The ship continued to Colombo, Aden, Naples, and Marseilles, finally arriving in London on 31 July 1899.

The voyage in the company of the swami was an education for Turiyananda and Nivedita. From beginning to end a vivid flow of thought and stories went on. One never knew what moment would bring the flash of intuition and the ringing utterance of some fresh truth. That encyclopedic mind touched all subjects: Christ, Buddha, Krishna, Ramakrishna, folklore, the history of India and Europe, the degradation of Hindu society and the assurance of its coming greatness, different philosophical and religious systems, and many themes more.

Sister Nivedita (previously Margaret Noble)

He was talking again, of the fact that he who would be great must suffer, and how some were fated to see every joy of the senses turn to ashes, and he said, "The whole of life is only a swan-song! Never forget those lines —

'The lion, when stricken to the heart, gives out his mightiest roar.
When smitten on the head, the cobra lifts its hood.
And the majesty of the soul comes forth only when a man is wounded to his depths.' "

— *Sister Nivedita*

Residence of Mrs. Samuel R. Noble (Nivedita's mother), Wimbledon (the four windows above "THE VILLAGE STORES")

To this voyage of six weeks I look back as the greatest occasion of my life. I missed no opportunity of the swami's society that presented itself, and accepted practically no other, filling up the time with quiet writing and needlework; thus I received one long continuous impression of his mind and personality, for which I can never be sufficiently thankful. . . .

It was while we sat chatting in the River [Ganges] on the first afternoon, that he suddenly exclaimed, "Yes! the older I grow, the more everything seems to me to lie in manliness. This is my new gospel." . . .

RICHMOND, NIVEDITA'S BROTHER, still in his teens, found in Swamiji a Christ-like man who could answer with authority his aching questions about human life and its meaning, about the existence of God and His ways to man. He found in Swamiji, moreover, a staunch ally against the tyranny of his elder sister. One day, Mlle. Lizelle Reymond recounts, the young Richmond jokingly complained (perhaps only half jokingly) that Nivedita, imposing Hindu customs upon her Irish family, had banned beef from the menus. Swamiji laughed. "So she has been laying down the law, has she!" Thereupon he took Richmond to a small restaurant and, to the young man's astonishment, ordered a beefsteak medium-rare (cuit à point, Mlle. Reymond's original French reads). "Eat, my boy," he said. "It's for you. I am giving you back what Nivedita has taken from you!"

Ridgely Manor, Stone Ridge, back view, ca. 1899

On the morning of Monday, 28 August 1899 the *S. S. Numidian* docked at New York, and once again, after an absence of almost three and a half years, Swami Vivekananda set foot on American soil. In New York, as in London, it was the off-season; thus that very afternoon, after visiting the townhouse of his old friends Mr. and Mrs. Francis Leggett, the swami and his brother disciple Swami Turiyananda went with them by train to Ridgely, their beautiful country home in the Hudson River Valley some ninety miles from New York.

The "Little Cottage" at Ridgely, front view (Swamis Vivekananda, Turiyananda, and Abhedananda were housed here.)

This "Little Cottage" (afterward always called "Swamiji's Cottage" by Miss MacLeod) contained five small bedrooms on the second floor, all with pitched ceilings. . . .

In connection with the swamis' sleeping quarters a charming story was told in later years by Miss MacLeod to Swami Nikhilananda, who passed it on to me [Marie Louise Burke]. Mrs. Leggett, coming to inspect the accommodations in the cottage, found Swami Turiyananda's mattress and bedding on the floor. . . ."What is the matter, Swami?" she exclaimed. "Is something wrong with the bed?" "No, no," he assured her; "the bed is fine. But, you see, I cannot bring myself to sleep on the same level with Swamiji — so I have put the mattress on the floor." One might add here that so great was the love and reverence that Swami Turiyananda always showed for Swamiji.

Ridgely Manor, 1899
Standing, left to right: *Swamis Vivekananda, Turiyananda, and Abhedananda.* Sitting, left to right: *Josephine MacLeod, a friend of Alberta's, Alberta Sturges, and Betty Leggett*

Ridgely Manor, 1899
Standing, left to right: *Swamis Turiyananda and Abhedananda.* Sitting, left to right: *Swami Vivekananda, Alberta Sturges, Betty Leggett (hidden), Josephine MacLeod, and a friend of Alberta's*

The outstanding impression made by the swami's bearing, during all these months of European and American life, was one of almost complete indifference to his surroundings. Current estimates of value left him entirely unaffected. He was never in any way startled or incredulous under success, being too deeply convinced of the greatness of the Power that worked through him, to be surprised by it. But neither was he unnerved by external failure. Both victory and defeat would come and go. He was their witness. . . .

He moved fearless and unhesitant through the luxury of the West. As determinedly as I had seen him in India, dressed in the two garments of simple folk, sitting on the floor and eating with his fingers, so, equally without doubt of shrinking, was his acceptance of the complexity of the means of living in America or France. Monk and king, he said, were obverse and reverse of a single medal. From the use of the best to the renunciation of all, was but one step. India had thrown all her prestige in the past, round poverty. Some prestige was in the future to be cast round wealth.

— *Sister Nivedita*

There are many memories connected with those days at Ridgely. Nearly every day Swami was wonderful in a new way! And now it would be music that he dwelt upon, now art, and once he burst into the morning-room, declaring for "Liberty." "What do I care if Mohammed *was* a good man, or Buddha! Does that alter *my* own goodness or evil? Let us be good for our own sake on our own responsibility! Not because somebody way back there was good!" Another time he tried to teach me an ancient Indian love song:

> And the flower says, nodding, nodding,
> Come gather me, and make of me a garland
> For the neck of thy beloved!

I could learn the words, but the air [tune] was quite beyond me, so full of little half-tones, and curious runs and turns.

— *Maud Stumm, a young American artist*

The dining room at Ridgely Manor

The Great Hall at Ridgely Manor

The swami used to call my sister, Mrs. Leggett, "Mother," and always sat beside her at table. He particularly liked chocolate ice cream, because, "I too am chocolate and I like it," he would say. One day we were having strawberries, and someone said to him, "Swami, do you like strawberries?" He answered, "I never tasted them." "You never tasted them, why you eat them every day!" He said, "You have cream on them — pebbles with cream would be good."

— *Josephine MacLeod*

One of the greatest things about swami was his human side. Like a big lovable boy, he thoroughly enjoyed the things he liked: ice cream, for example. How many times I have seen him rise from the table after salad, excusing himself to smoke or walk, when a very quick word from Lady Betty (Mrs. Francis H. Leggett) that she believed there was to be ice cream would turn him back instantly, and he would sink into his place with a smile of expectancy and pure delight seldom seen on the face of anybody over sixteen. He just loved it, and he had all he wanted, too.

— *Maud Stumm*

In the evening, sitting around the great fire in the hall of Ridgely Manor, he would talk, and once after he came out with some of his thoughts a lady said, "Swami, I don't agree with you there." "No? Then it is not for you," he answered. Someone else said, "Oh, but that is where I find you true." "Ah, then it was for you," he said showing that utter respect for the other man's views. One evening he was so eloquent, about a dozen people listening, his voice becoming so soft and seemingly far away; when the evening was over, we all separated without even saying goodnight to each other. Such a holy quality pervaded. My sister, Mrs. Leggett, had occasion to go to one of the rooms afterward. There she found one of the guests, an agnostic, weeping. "What do you mean?" my sister asked, and the lady said: "That man has given me eternal life. I never wish to hear him again."

— *Josephine MacLeod*

Vivekananda (pastel by Maud Stumm)

One day [at Ridgely] he told me that he wanted to undertake some sort of work that would keep his hands busy and prevent him from thinking of things that fretted him at that time — and would I give him drawing lessons? So materials were produced, and at an appointed hour he came, promptly, bringing to me, with a curious little air of submission, a huge red apple, which he laid in my hands, bowing gravely. I asked him the significance of this gift, and he said, "in token that the lessons may be fruitful" — and such a pupil as he proved to be! Once only did I have to tell him anything; his memory and concentration were marvellous, and his drawings strangely perfect and intelligent for a beginner. By the time he had taken his fourth lesson, he felt quite equal to a portrait. . . .

Then one very warm day, in the morning-room, we asked him to show us how he wound his turban and he did, adding several other methods employed by different castes and tribes. When he arranged it as the desert people do, to keep the neck from the great heat, I asked him to pose, and he did, talking all the time. That was the day he talked to us of purity and truth.

— *Maud Stumm*

London, 1895

AT ONE OF THE PUBLIC MEETINGS IN NEW YORK, after addressing a tense audience for about fifteen minutes, the swami suddenly made a formal bow and retired. The meeting broke up and the people went away greatly disappointed. A friend asked him, when he was returning home, why he had cut short the lecture in that manner, just when both he and the audience were warming up. Had he forgotten his points? Had he become nervous? The swami answered that at the meeting he had felt that he had too much power. He had noticed that the members of the audience were becoming so absorbed in his ideas that they were losing their own individualities. He had felt that they had become like soft clay and that he could give them any shape he wanted. That, however, was contrary to his philosophy. He wished every man and woman to grow according to his or her own inner law. He did not wish to change or destroy anyone's individuality. That was why he had had to stop.

Los Angeles, ca. 1890s

From New York Vivekananda arrived in Los Angeles via Chicago in the early afternoon of 3 December 1899 and became the guest of Mrs. S. K. Blodgett.

The impression the swami left in the mind of this good woman [Mrs. Blodgett] can be gathered from the following lines of a letter written by her to Miss MacLeod after Swamiji's passing away:

"I am ever recalling those swift, bright days in that never-to-be-forgotten winter, lived in simple freedom and kindliness. We could not choose but to be happy and good. . . . I knew him personally but a short time, yet in that time I could see in a hundred ways the child side of Swamiji's character, which was a constant appeal to the mother quality in all good women. . . . He would come home from a lecture, where he had been compelled to break away from his audience — so eagerly would they gather around him — and rush into the kitchen like a boy released from school, with 'Now we will cook!' Presently Joe would appear and discover the culprit among the pots and pans in his fine dress, who was admonished by thrifty, watchful Joe to change to his home garments. . . . In the homely old-fashioned kitchen, you and I have seen Swamiji at his best."

Mrs. Blodgett seldom went to hear him lecture, saying her duty was to give us delicious meals when we got back. Swami lectured a great number of times at the Home of Truth and in various halls [in Los Angeles], but perhaps the most outstanding lecture I ever heard was his talk on "Jesus of Nazareth" [actually "Christ, the Messenger"], when he seemed to radiate a white light from head to foot, so lost was he in the wonder and the power of Christ. I was so impressed with this obvious halo that I did not speak to him on the way back for fear of interrupting, as I thought, the great thoughts that were still in his mind. Suddenly he said to me, "I know how it is done." I said, "How what is done?" "How they make mulligatawny soup. They put a bay leaf in it," he told me. That utter lack of self-consciousness, of self-importance, was perhaps one of his outstanding characteristics.

— Josephine MacLeod

Josephine MacLeod

Swami Vivekananda was the guest of the Mead family of Pasadena for about six weeks in January and February 1900.

The [Mead] house stood at 309 Monterey Road in South Pasadena. It was a two-story frame house with gable roofs and a roofed-over front porch. Up the east end of the porch and over the roof grew a bushy Gold of Ophir rose vine, full of reddish yellow bloom. In this photograph one sees Swamiji standing at a corner of the house, the rose vine at his back, while Mrs. Wyckoff, standing on the porch, peeps from behind a pillar. . . .

The Mead household consisted of Mr. Mead, his three daughters, his two grandchildren — Mrs. Hansbrough's daughter, Dorothy, who was four years old, and Mrs. Wyckoff's son, Ralph, who was seventeen — and the housekeeper, Miss Fairbanks. How so many people could fit comfortably into so small a house is a marvel . . . .

The house, today owned by the Vedanta Society of Southern California and carefully restored to its original state, is surprisingly small. . . . Indeed, no visiting devotee would find it hard to think that Swamiji once walked through these rooms and filled this house through and through with his presence. . . .

South Pasadena (in front of the Mead's house), 1900

South Pasadena, 1900

"Often he would play with the children in the yard," Mrs. Hansbrough recalled. "Dorothy had several friends who would come, and he would hold hands with them and play ring-around-the-rosy and other games." No doubt Swamiji enjoyed these games for their own sake, as perfectly happy as his small companions; but he liked also to observe the ways of children and was interested in their early education. . . .

Ralph loved Swamiji and served him personally whenever and however he could. He would shine his shoes, fetch his tobacco from upstairs, and do other little things that Swamiji asked of him. Often they used to talk together, and Mrs. Hansbrough remembered that once Swamiji asked Ralph: "Can you see your own eyes?" Ralph answered that he could not, except in a mirror. "God is like that," Swamiji told him. "He is as close as your own eyes. He is your own, even though you can't see Him."

At a picnic, Pasadena, 1900
Vivekananda in centre; on his right, Mrs. Bruce; behind him, Carrie Wyckoff; on his left, Alice Hansbrough. The others are unknown.

After lunch Swamiji would generally recline on the couch in the living room, and there he would read or talk, while Mrs. Wyckoff busily pursued her various household tasks. "Madam," he one day said to her, "you work so hard that it makes me tired. Well, there have to be some Marthas, and you are a Martha," and sometimes he would ask her to stop her work and stroll with him in the garden. Strolling, he would sing Bengali songs or chant Sanskrit verses and "explain them," Mrs. Hansbrough tells us, "in a much more personal way than from the platform." Or sometimes he would sing the Christian hymn: "The heathen in his blindness bows down to wood and stone," the words of which Mrs. Hansbrough had taught him and which amused him greatly. "I am that heathen," he would laugh.

Often Swamiji would invite one person or another from his morning class to lunch at the Meads'. . . . But the best lunches of all were the picnics that took place on the open top of the nearby hill. . . . Mrs. Hansbrough said, "the air would become surcharged with a spiritual atmosphere." And she spoke of one occasion in particular when, absorbed in some subject he was discussing, "he talked for six hours without interruption — from ten in the morning until four in the afternoon." "The air," she said, "was just vibrant with spirituality by the time it was over." . . .

Unhappily, there are no known records of Swamiji's talks and informal classes on this sunny hilltop. Yet from a snatch of conversation that Mrs. Hansbrough remembered, it is clear that he was seeing all the world — its good and its evil alike — as a divine play, all supremely Good. On one of the picnics a young woman, a Christian Scientist, put forth the belief that one should teach people to be good. Swamiji smiled and waved his hand to indicate the trees and the countryside. "Why should I desire to be 'good'?" he asked. "All this is His handiwork. Shall I apologize for His handiwork? If you want to reform John Doe, go and live with him; don't try to reform him. If you have any of the Divine Fire, he will catch it."

At a picnic, Pasadena, 1900
Vivekananda in centre. Other picknickers are not identified.

The people of southern California were excursion-loving and the swami's hosts were no exception. Thus he was persuaded during his stay in Pasadena to make excursions here and there. There may not, however, have been many of these, for as Mrs. Hansbrough reminisced, he did not particularly care for sightseeing. "Once when we were up on the range of hills not far from our house," she relates, "my sister Helen was calling his attention to different views. 'Niece Helen,' said the swami, 'don't show me sights; I have seen the Himalayas! I would not go ten steps to see sights; but I would go a thousand miles to see a [great] human being!'"

In the second weekend of January, he made the trip up Mount Lowe, a high peak of the San Gabriel Range that rose just northwest of Pasadena. He was accompanied by Mr. and Mrs. Baumgardt, Miss MacLeod, and Mrs. Leggett, the last of whom had come to Los Angeles in early January. Part way up the mountain, the party stayed overnight at the then famous hotel called Echo Mountain House, where, on the morning of Sunday, 14 January, the swami gave a talk. That same day, he and his party proceeded to the summit of Mount Lowe via the tortuous but scenic Mount Lowe Railroad, and that evening, the excursion complete, they returned home.

Echo Mountain House Funicular, Mount Lowe, California, January 1900 (Vivekananda, second row, fifth from left)

Echo Mountain House, Mount Lowe

I WAS ONCE TRAVELLING IN THE HIMALAYAS, and the long road stretched before us. We poor monks cannot get anyone to carry us, so we had to make all the way on foot. There was an old man with us. The way goes up and down for hundreds of miles, and when that old monk saw what was before him, he said, "Oh, sir, how to cross it; I cannot walk anymore; my chest will break." I said to him, "Look down at your feet." He did so, and I said, "The road that is under your feet is the road that you have passed over and is the same road that you see before you; it will soon be under your feet." The highest things are under your feet because you are Divine Stars; all these things are under your feet. You can swallow the stars by the handful if you want; such is your real nature. Be strong, get beyond all superstitions, and be free.

— *Vivekananda*

Universalist Church, Pasadena

Assembly Hall, Shakespeare Club, Pasadena, 1900

Take the Bible, for instance, and all the sects that exist amongst Christians; each one puts its own interpretation upon the same text, and each says that it alone understands that text and all the rest are wrong. So with every religion. There are many sects among the Mohammedans and among the Buddhists, and hundreds among the Hindus. Now, I bring these facts before you in order to show you that any attempt to bring all humanity to one method of thinking in spiritual things has been a failure and always will be a failure. . . .

I am not against any sect. I am glad that sects exist, and I only wish they may go on multiplying more and more. Why? Simply because of this: If you and I and all who are present here were to think exactly the same thoughts, there would be no thoughts for us to think. We know that two or more forces must come into collision in order to produce motion. It is the clash of thought, the differentiation of thought, that awakes thought. Now, if we all thought alike, we would be like Egyptian mummies in a museum looking vacantly at one another's faces — no more than that! Whirls and eddies occur only in a rushing, living stream. There are no whirlpools in stagnant, dead water. When religions are dead, there will be no more sects; it will be the perfect peace and harmony of the grave. But so long as mankind thinks, there will be sects. Variation is the sign of life, and it must be there. I pray that they may multiply so that at last there will be as many sects as human beings, and each one will have his own method, his individual method of thought in religion.

HINDUISM HAS THIS ADVANTAGE: its secret is that doctrines and dogmas do not mean anything; what you are is what matters. If you talk all the best philosophies the world ever produced, [but] if you are a fool in your behaviour, they do not count; and if in your behaviour you are good, you have more chances. . . .

The Vedantist has patience to wait for everybody. Wherever you are, this is the highest: "I and my Father are one." Realize it. If an image helps, images are welcome. If worshipping a great man helps you, worship him. If worshipping Mohammed helps you, go on. Only be sincere; and if you are sincere, says Vedantism, you are sure to be brought to the goal. None will be left. Your heart, which contains all truth, will unfold itself chapter after chapter, till you know the last truth, that "I and my Father are one." And what is salvation? To live with God. Where? Anywhere. Here this moment. One moment in infinite time is quite as good as any other moment. This is the old doctrine of the Vedas, you see.

— *Vivekananda*

From Los Angeles he [Swamiji] came to San Francisco in February 1900, and his first [actually his second] public lecture in Oakland was given on 28 February 1900 in the Unitarian Church, Oakland, of which church the Reverend Benjamin Fay Mills was the pastor. The subject of this lecture was "Similarity between the Vedanta Philosophy and Christianity." He told us always to look for similarities, for common points of interest, and never to look for differences. I was at that lecture, and the impression he made on me was, "Here is a man who *knows* what he is talking about. He is not repeating what some other person told him. He is not relating what he thinks, he is telling what he knows." Going home from the lecture I was walking on air. When I got home I was still acting like a crazy man. When I was asked what sort of a man he was, I replied, "He is not a man, he is a god." I can never forget the impression he produced on me. To me he was a wonder, and I followed him to any of the Bay cities where he spoke.

— *Thomas J. Allan*

San Francisco, 1900

First Unitarian Church, Oakland, California, ca. 1900

"After the lecture was over," Miss [Sarah] Fox went on, "the swami invited questions, and the one which I remember was particularly foolish. An unlucky woman asked, 'Is it true, swami? I have heard that you throw newborn babies into the Ganges.' The swami replied, 'Madam, we have heard that at Thanksgiving you serve newborn babies!'"

(Swamiji seems never to have run out of answers to this question, which pursued him from one end of the United States to the other. In Los Angeles he had replied, "Yes, madam; but I was one who escaped." Or, when the question applied to girl babies only: "Yes, madam, and nowadays all the babies are born of men." And in Detroit in 1894 when he was asked why only female children were given to the crocodiles, he had answered, "Probably because they are softer and more tender and can be more easily masticated." Or again in Detroit: "I was such a fat little baby the crocodiles refused to swallow me. Whenever I feel badly about being such a fat monk, I think of how I was saved from the crocodiles and am comforted." And in Minneapolis, "Yes, madam, they threw me in, but like your fabled Jonah, I got out again." Thus he ridiculed stupidity until it hid its head in shame — literally.)

San Francisco, 1900

Francis (Frank) Sprague Rhodehamel in later years

What becomes of one's individuality when one realizes his oneness with God? "You people in this country are so afraid of losing your in-di-vid-u-al-i-ty!" he would exclaim. "Why, you are not individuals yet. When you realize your whole nature, you will attain your true individuality, not before. In knowing God you cannot lose anything. There is another thing I am constantly hearing in this country, and that is that we should live in harmony with nature. Don't you know that all the progress ever made in the world was made by conquering nature? We are to resist nature at every point if we are to make any progress."

He encouraged questions at the end of each lecture, and once when someone suggested that they were tiring him with too many questions, he said, "Ask all the questions you like, the more the better. That is what I am here for and I won't leave you until you understand. In India they tell me, I ought not to teach Advaita (monistic) Vedanta to the people at large, but I say I can make even a child understand it. You cannot begin too early to teach the highest spiritual truths."

— *Ida Ansell*

It is now more than ten years since Swami Vivekananda lectured to California audiences; it seems but yesterday. It was here as elsewhere; the audiences were his from the outset and remained his to the end. They were swept along on the current of his thought without resistance.

The swami's personality impressed itself on the mind with visual intensity. The speaking eyes, the wealth of facial expression, and gesticulation; the wondrous Sanskrit chanting, sonorous, melodious, impressing one with the sense of mystic potency; the translations following in smiling confidence — all these, set off by the spectacular apparel of the Hindu sannyasin — who can forget them?

As a lecturer he was unique: never referring to notes, as most lecturers do; and though he repeated many discourses on request, they were never mere repetitions. He seemed to be giving something of himself, to be speaking from a superexperience. The most abstruse points of the Vedanta were retrieved from the domain of mere speculation by a vital something which seemed to emanate from him. His utterances were dynamic and constructive: arousing thought and directing it into synthetic process. Thus he was not only a lecturer but a Teacher of the highest order as well.

— *Francis Rhodehamel*

Edith B. Allan, ca. 1902

Thomas J. Allan, ca. 1907

I attended all Swamiji's public lectures both in San Francisco and Alameda, it was this close contact with Swamiji that I most deeply cherish. Once after being quiet for some time Swamiji said, "Madame, be broad-minded, always see two ways. When I am on the Heights I say 'I am He,' and when I have a stomachache, I say 'Mother, have mercy on me.' Always see two ways." On another occasion he said: "Learn to be the witness. If there are two dogs fighting on the street and I go out there, I get mixed up in the fight; but if I stay quietly in my room, I witness the fight from the window. So learn to be the witness." While in Alameda Swamiji gave public lectures in Tucker Hall. He gave one wonderful lecture "The Ultimate Destiny of Man" and finished by placing his hand on his chest and saying "I am God." A most awed silence fell upon the audience, and many people thought it blasphemy for Swamiji to say such a thing. . . .

Swamiji was not in good health — much lecturing told upon him. He used to say he did not like platform work, "Public lecturing is killing. At eight o'clock I am to speak on 'Love.' At eight o'clock I do not feel like love!"

— *Edith Allan*

Swamiji's lecture on "Sri Krishna and His Message" was scheduled on 25 March 1900 at 3 p.m. at Union Square Hall, San Francisco.

"At 3 p.m.," Mr. Allan wrote in his memoirs, "Swami was not there. We waited and wondered what to do, and concluded that we must just wait." But Mr. Allan, who acted now as head usher at all of Swamiji's lectures, did not just wait. He walked from the hall to the corner of Post and Powell streets, looked up and down Powell Street, waited awhile, saw no sign of Swamiji, and returned to the hall. This he did several times. It was probably not until his fourth or fifth trip to the corner that he saw Swamiji walking slowly up Powell Street in his own composed and majestic rhythm. The time was then three-thirty. But Mr. Allan's difficulties were not over. "I met him at the corner of Post Street," he continued in his memoirs, "and walked with him towards the hall." (According to Mr. Brown, who had often heard the story from Mr. Allan, the latter had said, "Swami, don't you know you're late? The audience has been waiting." To which Swamiji had replied, "Mr. Allan, I am never late. I have all the time in the world. All time is mine." "Well, swami," Mr. Allan said, "the audience may not feel the same as you do." But Swamiji just went on at his same leisurely pace.) "On the way we had to pass a shoe-shine stand," Mr. Allan's memoirs continue, "and when Swami saw that, and saw that the shoe-shiner was idle, he decided to have his shoes shined. Did I not silently fidget, remembering the people who had come to hear the lecture! But all my fidgeting did no good. Well, at last, Swami got on the platform and was introduced to that audience, which had more or less patiently waited for him."

San Francisco, 1900

In this country [America] the king has entered every one of you. You are all kings in this country. So with the religion of Vedanta. You are all Gods. One God is not sufficient. You are all Gods, says the Vedanta.

This makes Vedanta very difficult. It does not teach the old idea of God at all. In place of that God who sat above the clouds and managed the affairs of the world without asking our permission, who created us out of nothing, just because He liked it, and made us undergo all this misery, just because He liked it, Vedanta teaches the God that is in everyone, has become everyone and everything. His majesty the king has gone from this country; the Kingdom of Heaven went from Vedanta hundreds of years ago. . . . There is a chance of Vedanta becoming the religion of your country because of democracy. But it can become

San Francisco, 1900

so only if you can and do clearly understand it, if you become real men and women, not people with vague ideas and superstitions in your brains, and if you want to be truly spiritual, since Vedanta is concerned only with spirituality. . . .

These are what Vedanta has not to give. No book. No man to be singled out from the rest of mankind — "You are worms, and we are the Lord God!" — none of that. If you are the Lord God, I also am the Lord God. So Vedanta knows no sin. There are mistakes, but no sin; and in the long run everything is going to be all right. No Satan — none of this nonsense. Vedanta believes in only one sin, only one in the world, and it is this: the moment you think you are a sinner, or anybody is a sinner, that is sin. From that follows every other mistake, or what is usually called sin. There have been many mistakes in our lives. But we are going on. Glory be unto us that we have made mistakes! Take a long look at your past life. If your present condition is good, it has been caused by all the past mistakes as well as successes. Glory be unto success! Glory be unto mistakes! Do not look back upon what has been done. Go ahead! . . .

San Francisco, 1900

No book, no person, no Personal God. All these must go. Again, the senses must go. We cannot be bound to the senses. At present we are tied down — like persons dying of cold in the glaciers. They feel such a strong desire to sleep, and when their friends try to wake them, warning them of death, they say, "Let me die, I want to sleep." We all cling to the little things of the senses, even if we are ruined thereby: we forget there are much greater things.

— *Vivekananda*

Once at the conclusion of a lecture he thus announced his next lecture: "Tomorrow night I shall lecture on 'The Mind: Its Powers and Possibilities.' Come to hear me. I have something to say to you, I shall do a little bomb-throwing." Here he glanced smilingly over the audience, and then with a wave of his hand added, "Come on! It will do you good." The next night there was barely standing-room. He kept his word. Bombs were thrown, and he, of all people, knew how to throw them with telling effect. In this lecture he devoted considerable time to the subject of chastity as a means of strengthening the mind. As a practice to develop purity, he expounded the theory of looking upon every woman as one's mother. . . .

"Don't repent! Don't repent! . . . Spit, if you must, but go on! Don't hold yourselves down by repenting! Throw off the load of sin, if there is such a thing, by knowing your true selves — The Pure! The Ever Free! . . . That man alone is blasphemous who tells you that you are sinners. . . ." And again: "This world is a superstition. We are hypnotized into believing it real. The process of salvation is the process of dehypnotization. . . . This universe is just the play of the Lord — that is all. It is all just for fun. There can be no reason for His doing anything. Know the Lord if you would understand His play. Be His playfellow, and He will tell you all."

Stand up and fight! Not one step back, that is the idea. . . . Fight it out, whatever comes. Let the stars move from the spheres! Let the whole world stand against us! Death means only a change of garment. What of it? Thus fight! You gain nothing by becoming cowards. . . . Taking a step backward, you do not avoid any misfortune. You have cried to all the gods in the world. Has misery ceased? The masses in India cry to sixty million gods, and still die like dogs. Where are these gods? . . . The gods come to help you when you have succeeded. So what is the use? Die game. . . . This bending the knee to superstitions, this selling yourself to your own mind, does not befit you, my soul. You are infinite, deathless, birthless. Because you are infinite spirit, it does not befit you to be a slave. . . . Arise! Awake! Stand up and fight! Die if you must. There is none to help you. You are all the world. Who can help you?

— *Vivekananda*

San Francisco, 1900

Alameda, 1900

His simple fun-loving nature carried his hearers along with him in the spirit of his joke. At another time: "The Christian idea of hell is not at all terrifying to me. I have read Dante's *Inferno* three times, but I must say that I find nothing terrible in it. There are many kinds of Hindu hells. When a glutton dies, for instance, he is surrounded by great quantities of the very best kinds of food. He has a stomach a thousand miles long, and a mouth as small as a pin-head! Think of that!" During this lecture he got very warm owing to the poor ventilation. On leaving the hall after the lecture, he was met by a chill blast of north wind. Gathering his coat tightly about him he said vehemently, "Well, if *this* isn't hell, I don't know what is."

On another occasion, while speaking seriously, he suddenly broke out in merriment: "As soon as a man gets a little sense he dies. He begins by having a big stomach which sticks out farther than his head. When he gains wisdom, his stomach disappears and his head becomes prominent. Then he dies."

The swami was blessed with an irrepressible sense of humour, which enlivened his lectures and classes, and at times relieved the tenseness of embarrassing situations. Observe his parry to the question incredulously hurled at him at the close of a lecture which culminated in an impassioned outburst on the glory of God-Consciousness: "Swami, have you seen God?" "What!" he returned, his face lighting up with a happy smile, "Do I look like it — a big fat man like me?"

On another occasion while he was expounding Advaita, an old man, sitting in the front row, arose deliberately, and with a look which said as plainly as words, "Let me get out of this place in a hurry," hobbled down the aisle and out of the hall, pounding the floor with his cane at every step. The swami apparently enjoyed the situation, for amusement overspread his features as he paused to watch him. The attention of the audience was divided between the swami, smiling, fun-loving, and the disgusted old man who had had enough of him. . . .

Alameda, 1900

Speaking of spiritual training for the mind, he said, "The less you read the better. What are books but the vomitings of other men's minds? Why fill your mind with a load of stuff you will have to get rid of? Read the Gita and other good works on Vedanta. That is all you need." Then again: "The present system of education is all wrong. The mind is crammed with facts before it knows how to think. Control of the mind should be taught first. If I had my education to get over again, and had any voice in the matter, I would learn to master my mind first, and then gather facts, if I wanted them. It takes people a long time to learn things, because they can't concentrate their minds at will. . . . It took three readings for me to memorize Macaulay's *History of England*, while my mother memorized any sacred book in only one reading. . . . People are always suffering because they can't control their minds. To give an illustration, though a rather crude one: a man has trouble with his wife. She leaves him and goes with other men. She's a terror! But, poor fellow, he can't take his mind away from her, and so he suffers."

Washington Hall, Red Men's Building, San Francisco, ca. 1900 (third building from right)

San Francisco, 1900

IN SAN FRANCISCO, AS ELSEWHERE, the swami's towering and benign personality stood before his listeners as irrefutable proof of his message. There he was — a man who was himself Godlike, who clearly had realized what he preached, and who could transport others into that same divine awareness. Whether his health was good or bad made no difference to this power of his. So friendly and simple was the swami that those who were close to him sometimes forgot his gigantic dimensions. Reminders, however, would flash out. Mr. Thomas Allan, whose first experience of him had convinced him that he had heard "not a man, but a God," soon became his close follower and an usher at his lectures. He was again to be awed by a sudden awareness that the swami was far bigger than life: "It was when I introduced him at [a Sunday] lecture," he later recalled, "that I felt like a pygmy and saw him as an immense giant. After this experience I could not bring myself to stand beside him again, but always thereafter made my introduction from the foot of the platform."

On 22 April [1900], Miss Bell, Mrs. Roorbach, and I were established at Camp Irving (the name of Mr. Juhl's camp at the outskirts of Camp Taylor, a rustic summer retreat in Marin County) a few miles north of San Francisco. The campground was a narrow strip of land between a railroad track and a creek. There was a circular clump of trees at one end which we used as a sort of chapel for classes and meditation. The kitchen was at the other end and its equipment consisted of a stove under a tree, a trunk for supplies, a rough board table with benches on either side, and some shelves built into the tree for dishes, the pots and pans being hung on nails driven into the tree. Between these two provisions for spiritual and material food there was room for four tents and an open space for a campfire. . . .

During one of the talks in Miss Bell's tent at Camp Irving, Miss Bell remarked that the world is a school where we come to learn our lesson. Swamiji asked, "Who told you that the world is a school?"

Kitchen at Camp Irving, August 1900
(Seated: Mrs. R. N. Miller; at stove: Eloise Roorbach)

Left to right: Emily Aspinall, Mrs. Schultz, Lydia Bell, Ida Ansell, and Eloise Roorbach

Miss Bell was silent. Swamiji went on, "This world is a circus, and we are clowns come to tumble." Miss Bell asked, "Why do we tumble, Swamiji?" Swamiji replied: "Because we like to tumble. When we get tired of tumbling, we quit."

— *Ida Ansell*

"Mrs. Hansbrough thought Swamiji should rest," Mrs. Allan wrote, "as he had done so much lecturing and should not be asked to talk or meditate with the students, but Miss Bell wanted him to do so, and he acquiesced. Mrs. Hansbrough did not attend these meetings. One morning when the other students had gathered in the tent Swamiji went into the open-air kitchen and asked if she was not coming to meditation. She replied: 'I can't come just yet; I'm busy cooking. I'll come later.' Swamiji said, 'That's all right, you do not need to meditate; I'll meditate for you.'" (One finds this not improbable repetition of an incident that occurred in the Turk Street flat also told in Miss Ansell's published memoirs in connection with Camp Taylor. There, however, one reads that Swamiji excused Mrs. Hansbrough with the words, "Well, never mind; our Master said you could leave meditation for service.")

Mary Hale, ca. 1896

Early photograph taken in America (place and date unknown)

I am free — therefore I require none else for my happiness. Alone through eternity — because I was free, am free, and shall remain free forever. This is Vedantism. I preached the theory so long, but oh, joy! Mary, my dear sister, I am realizing it now every day. Yes, I am. I am free. Alone — Alone — I am the One without a second.

Now I am going to be truly Vivekananda. Did you ever enjoy evil? Ha, ha — you silly girl — awl is goood! Nonsense — some good, some evil. I enjoy the good and I enjoy the evil. I was Jesus and I was Judas Iscariot, both — my play, my fun. "So long as there are two, fear shall not leave thee." Ostrich method? Hide your heads in the sand? — and think there is nobody seeing you! Awl is goood! Be brave and face everything. Come, good; come, evil — both welcome — both of you my play. I have no good to attain, no ideal to clinch up to, no ambition to fulfill. I, the diamond mine, am playing with pebbles, good and evil. Good for you, evil, come; good for you, good, you come too. If the universe tumbles round my ears, what is that to me? I am Peace that passeth understanding. Understanding only gives us good or evil. I am beyond — I am *Peace.*

— *Vivekananda*

During his trip back to New York, across the American continent, the swami was very much fatigued. He stopped in Chicago and Detroit on the way. In Chicago he was the guest of the Hale family, and many old reminiscences were exchanged. On the morning of his departure, Mary came to the swami's room and found him sad. His bed appeared to have been untouched, and on being asked the reason, he confessed that he had spent the whole night without sleep. "Oh," he said, almost in a whisper, "it is so difficult to break human bonds!" He knew that this was the last time he was to visit these devoted friends.

Sister Devamata (Laura Glenn)

Sister Devamata described Swamiji at the breakfast table one July morning designing the emblem that was later to become the seal of the Ramakrishna Order and that is today so familiar to readers of the Order's literature. She wrote of the incident in her Memories of India and Indians, *first published serially in* Prabuddha Bharata *of 1932. (In 1896 Sister Devamata — then Laura Glenn — had regularly attended Swamiji's New York lectures and classes. She received her monastic name years later from Swami Paramananda.)*

The design which has become the symbol of the Ramakrishna Mission everywhere [she wrote in her *Memories*] came into being in the same casual way as did the "Song of the Sannyasin." It took shape in 1900 during Swami Vivekananda's later visit to America. At that time the Vedanta Society of New York was definitely established and occupied a modest house on Fifty-eighth Street. Mrs. Crane, the housekeeper, told me that the swami was sitting at the breakfast table one morning when the printer arrived. He said he was making a circular for the Society and wished to have an emblem to go on it, could the swami suggest something? Swamiji took the envelope from a letter he had just received, tore it open and on the clean inner surface drew the waves, the swan, the lotus, and the sun circled by a serpent — the four Yogas wrapped about by eternity, it seemed. He threw the bit of paper with the design on it across the table and said, 'Draw it to scale.' Henry van Haagen, the printer, was an able draughtsman as well as printer. He converted the rough sketch into a finished drawing."

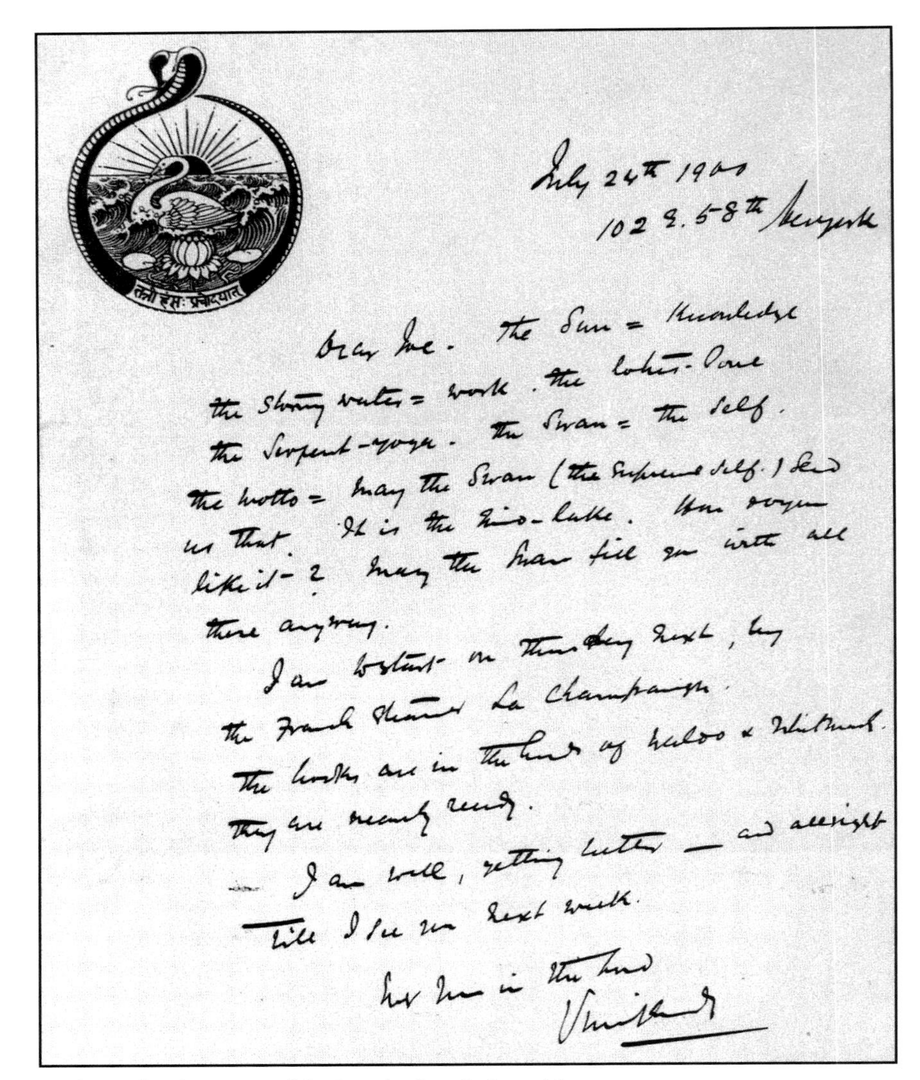

July 24th 1900
102 E. 58th Newyork

Dear Joe. The Sun = Knowledge
the Stormy water = work. the lotus = Love
the Serpent - yoga. the Swan = the Self.
the motto = May the Swan (the Supreme Self.) Send
us That. It is the mind-lake. How do you
like it - ? May the Swan fill you with all
these anyway.

I am to start on Thursday next, by
the French Steamer La Champagne.
The books are in the hands of Waldo & Whitmarsh.
They are nearly ready.

I am well, getting better — and allright
— Till I see you next week.

Ever Yours in the Lord
Vivekananda

Vivekananda's description of the Ramakrishna Order emblem

Later on in India Swamiji again explained the significance of the design, this time to the artist Ranadaprasad Das Gupta. "The wavy waters in the picture are symbolic of Karma," he said; "the lotus, of Bhakti; and the rising-sun, of Jnana. The encircling serpent is indicative of Yoga and the awakened Kundalini Shakti, while the swan in the picture stands for the Paramatman (Supreme Self). Therefore, the idea of the picture is that by the union of Karma, Jnana, Bhakti, and Yoga, the vision of the Paramatman is obtained."

"Well, Brother, my days are numbered," Swamiji had said to Swami Abhedananda. "I shall live only for three or four years at the most." "You must not talk like that, Swamiji," Swami Abhedananda had remonstrated. "You are fast recovering your health. . . ." But Swamiji had replied, "You do not understand me. I feel that I am growing very big. My self is expanding so much that at times I feel as if this body could not contain me anymore. I am about to burst. Surely, this cage of flesh and blood cannot hold me for many days more."

Leggett residence (centre house), 6 Place des Etats-Unis, Paris

Swami Abhedananda in America

ON THE AFTERNOON OF FRIDAY, 3 August 1900, the *S. S. Champagne*, which Swamiji had boarded in New York on 26 July 1900, docked at Le Havre. Several hours later (at eight o'clock, according to his telegram to Mrs. Francis Leggett) he arrived at the Saint-Lazare station in Paris, the "capital of modern civilization."

In the second part of his *Memoirs of European Travel* Swamiji wrote (originally in Bengali) of "the daily reunion of numbers of distinguished men and women which Mr. Leggett brought about at an enormous expense in his Parisian mansion, by inviting them to at-homes. . . .

"All types of distinguished personages — poets, philosophers, scientists, moralists, politicians, singers, professors, painters, artists, sculptors, musicians, and so on, of both sexes — used to be assembled in Mr. Leggett's residence, attracted by his hospitality and kindness," he related. "That incessant outflow of words, clear and limpid like a mountain-fall, that expression of sentiments emanating from all sides like sparks of fire, bewitching music, the magic current of thought from masterminds coming into conflict with one another . . . used to hold all spellbound, making them forgetful of time and place."

Eiffel Tower surrounded by Paris Exposition, 1900

The main event of his stay in Paris was his appearance at the Congress of the History of Religions, which was held from September 3 through 8, 1900, at the Sorbonne in connection with the Paris Exposition. . . .

Being scheduled to speak on 7 September he was present when a paper was read that morning by a Mr. Gustav Oppert, a German Orientalist, who tried to trace the origin of the Shalagrama-Shila and the Shiva-Linga to mere phallicism. To this the swami objected, adducing proofs from the Vedas, and particularly the Atharva-Veda Samhita, to the effect that the Shiva-Linga had its origin in the idea of the Yupa-Stambha or Skambha, the sacrificial post idealized in Vedic ritual as the symbol of the Eternal Brahman.

The Shalagrama-Shilas were natural stones, resembling the artificially cut stones of the Dhatu-Garbha, or "metal-wombed," stone reliquaries of the Bauddha Stupas, and these, being first worshipped by the Buddhists, gradually found their way into Vaishnavism. The explanation of the Shalagrama-Shila as a phallic emblem was an imaginary invention. A degenerate period in India, following the downfall of Buddhism, had brought on the association of sex with the Shiva-Linga. In reality, the Shiva-Linga and the Shalagrama-Shila had no more to do with sex-worship than the Holy Communion in Christianity had in common with cannibalism.

By all accounts the Exposition of 1900 was indeed a grand affair. It cost a hundred million francs. It covered about 250 acres in central Paris. There were art exhibits in the Grand Palais; and in the Petit Palais art in industry was displayed. Big buildings on the Champ-de-Mars displayed the latest machines and industrial products. Foreign countries gave an international aspect to the exposition by building, along the Seine River, pavilions designed to recall the best architecture of their lands. There were fountains and monumental archways. In the centre of all this stood the then new Eiffel Tower, the tallest structure in the world. . . . Much of the walking of long distances — always a problem with big expositions — was reduced by the presence of marvellous moving sidewalks. . . .

Paris Exposition, 1900

Mrs. Frances Leggett wrote: "My half-sister Alberta [Alberta Sturges, daughter of Mrs. F. H. Leggett, Sr. by her first marriage] told me that she, Swami, and my father went every morning to see the Exhibition, accompanied by Professor Patrick Geddes, who explained to them the exhibits." From a letter Josephine MacLeod wrote to Sara Bull we know that on 4 August 1900, Swamiji was to have had dinner in the restaurant of the Eiffel Tower with Josephine MacLeod, Sister Nivedita, and a friend of the Leggetts who lived in Paris, Gerald Nobel.

The former salon of the Leggetts' Paris house

In Paris Swami Vivekananda was the guest of Mr. and Mrs. Leggett, at whose house he met many distinguished people. Among these was the young Duke of Richelieu, a scion of an old and aristocratic family of France. The title had been created by Louis XIII, and one of the ancestors of the Duke had been Premier under Louis XVIII. Born in Paris, educated at a Jesuit school in France, and later graduated from the University of Aix-en-Provence, the Duke of Richelieu became greatly attached to the swami and visited him frequently. On the eve of Vivekananda's departure from Paris, the swami asked the Duke if he would renounce the world and become his disciple. The Duke wanted to know what he would gain in return for such renunciation, and the swami said, "I shall give you the desire for death." When asked to explain, the swami declared that he would give the Duke such a state of mind that when confronted by death he would laugh at it. But the Duke preferred to pursue a worldly career, though he cherished a lifelong devotion to Swami Vivekananda.

From Paris our friend Maxim has supplied me with letters of introduction to various places, so that the countries may be properly seen. Maxim is the inventor of the famous Maxim gun — the gun that sends off a continuous round of balls and is loaded and discharged automatically without intermission. Maxim is by birth an American; now he has settled in England, where he has his gun-factories, etc. Maxim is vexed if anybody alludes too frequently to his guns in his presence and says, "My friend, have I done nothing else except invent that engine of destruction?" Maxim is an admirer of China and India and is a good writer on religion and philosophy, etc. Having read my works long since, he holds me in great — I should say, excessive — admiration. He supplies guns to all kings and rulers and is well-known in every country.

— *Vivekananda*

Sir Hiram Maxim

Orient Express Poster

After staying almost three months in France, the swami toured some European countries as the guest of Madame Emma Calvé. He wrote in his Memoirs of European Travel:

The tour programme was as follows — from Paris to Vienna, and thence to Constantinople, by rail; then by steamer to Athens and Greece, then across the Mediterranean to Egypt, then Asia Minor, Jerusalem, and so on. The "Oriental Express" runs daily from Paris to Constantinople, and is provided with sleeping, sitting, and dining accommodations after the American model. Though not perfect like the American cars, they are fairly well furnished. I am to leave Paris by that train on 24 October 1900.

⁂

I have three travelling companions — two of them French and the third an American. The American is Miss MacLeod; the French male companion is Monsieur Jules Bois, a famous philosopher and litterateur of France; and the French lady friend is the world-renowned singer, Mademoiselle Calvé. . . .

We have two other companions on the journey as far as Constantinople — Pére Hyacinthe and his wife. Pére, i.e., Father Hyacinthe, was a monk of a strict ascetic section of the Roman Catholic Church. His scholarship, extraordinary eloquence, and great austerities own for him a high reputation in France and in the whole Catholic Order. . . . At forty years of age Pére Hyacinthe fell in love with an American woman and eventually married her. This created a great sensation, and of course the Catholic Order immediately gave him up. Discarding his ascetic garb of bare feet and loose-fitting cloak, Pére Hyacinthe took up the hat, coat, and boots of the householder and became — Monsieur Loyson. . . . Old Loyson is very affable in speech, modest, and of a distinctly devotional turn of mind. Whenever he meets me, he holds pretty long talks about various religions and creeds. But being of a devotional temperament, he is a little afraid of the Advaita [Nondualistic Vedanta].

— *Vivekananda*

Pére Hyacinthe Loyson, 1905

What a pilgrimage it was! Science, philosophy, and history had no secrets from the swami. I listened with all my ears to the wise and learned discourse that went on around me. I did not attempt to join in their arguments, but I sang on all occasions, as is my custom. The swami would discuss all sorts of questions with Father Loyson, who was a scholar and a theologian of repute. It was interesting to see that the swami was able to give the exact text of a document, the date of a Church Council, when Father Loyson himself was not certain.

When we were in Greece, we visited Eleusis. He explained its mysteries to us and led us from altar to altar, from temple to temple, describing the processions that were held in each place, intoning the ancient prayers, showing us the priestly rites.

A street scene in Cairo, Egypt

Later, in Egypt, one unforgettable night, he led us again into the past, speaking to us in mystic, moving words, under the shadow of the silent sphinx.

The swami was always absorbingly interesting, even under ordinary conditions. He fascinated his hearers with his magic tongue. Again and again we would miss our train, sitting calmly in a station waiting room, enthralled by his discourse and quite oblivious of the lapse of time. Even Miss MacLeod, the most sensible among us, would forget the hour, and we would in consequence find ourselves stranded far from our destination at the most inconvenient times and places.

One day we lost our way in Cairo. I suppose we had been talking too intently. At any rate, we found ourselves in a squalid, ill-smelling street, where half-clad women lolled from windows and sprawled on doorsteps.

The swami noticed nothing until a particularly noisy group of women on a bench in the shadow of a dilapidated building began laughing and calling to him. One of the ladies of our party tried to hurry us along, but the swami detached himself gently from our group and approached the women on the bench.

Josephine MacLeod and Emma Calvé

"Poor children!" he said. "Poor creatures! They have put their divinity in their beauty. Look at them now!"

He began to weep. The women were silenced and abashed. One of them leaned forward and kissed the hem of his robe, murmuring brokenly in Spanish, "Humbre de Dios, Humbre de Dios!" (Man of God!). Another, with a sudden gesture of modesty and fear, threw her arm in front of her face as though she would screen her shrinking soul from those pure eyes.

This marvellous journey proved to be almost the last occasion on which I was to see the swami. Shortly afterward he announced that he was to return to his own country. He felt that his end was approaching, and he wished to go back to the community of which he was director and where he had spent his youth.

— Emma Calvé ❧

London, 1895

IX

"I Shall Never See Forty"

Vivekananda arrived at Belur Math unannounced on 9 December 1900. His brother monks and disciples were jubilant to have their leader back. Later, Vivekananda received the sad news of Mr. Sevier's passing away. On 27 December he left for Mayavati in the Himalayas to console Mrs. Sevier, arriving there on 3 January 1901. It was a severe winter. He stayed there for a couple of weeks and then returned to Belur Math on 24 January.

During this time the swami received invitations for a lecture tour in East Bengal (now Bangladesh), and his mother also expressed a desire to visit the holy places in that part of the country. On 26 January he wrote to Mrs. Ole Bull: "I am going to take my mother on pilgrimage. . . . This is the one great wish of a Hindu widow. I have only brought misery to my people all my life. I am trying to fulfill this one wish of hers."

On 18 March the swami, in spite of his poor health, left for Dhaka with a large party. He exhorted the people of Dhaka to cultivate manliness and the faculty of reasoning. To a sentimental young man he said: "My boy, take my advice: develop your muscles and brain by eating good food and by healthy exercise, and then you will be able to think for yourself." On another occasion, addressing the youths of Bengal, who had very little physical stamina, he said, "You will be nearer to God through football than through the Bhagavad Gita."

He returned to Belur Math on 12 May. Vivekananda tried to lead a carefree life at the monastery — sometimes talking to the poor labourers who were levelling the ground, sometimes supervising the cooking arrangements, sometimes singing devotional songs with the monks. At other times he imparted spiritual instructions to visitors, or engaged in meditation or serious study.

He continued to train his disciples: "In every country, nations have their good and bad sides. Ours is to do good works in our lives and hold an example before others. No work succeeds by condemnation. It only repels people. Let anybody say what he likes, don't contradict him. In this world of maya, whatever work you will take up will be attended with some defect. 'All undertakings are beset with imperfections, as fire with smoke.' [Gita, XVIII. 48] But will you, on that account, sit inactive? As far as you can, you must go on doing good work."

His fragile body could not dampen his spirit to work. When urged to rest, he said to a disciple: "My son, there is no rest for me. That which Sri Ramakrishna called 'Kali' took possession of my body and soul three or four days before his passing away. That makes me work and work and never lets me keep still or look to my personal comfort."

At last the final day came: 4 July 1902. He meditated three hours that morning, conducted a class on Sanskrit grammar and Vedanta philosophy for the monks in the afternoon, and then took a long walk with Swami Premananda. At dusk he took a cup of tea. Then while going to his room he said to Bodhananda, "See that they [monks] all get new mosquito curtains." He was concerned that the monks might suffer from malaria. He went to his room and said to his attendant, "Wait and meditate till I call you." He himself sat for meditation and gave up his body through samadhi.

Old Belur Math building (shrine upstairs)

On 19 December 1900, he wrote to a Western disciple: "Verily I am a bird of passage. Gay and busy Paris, grim old Constantinople, sparkling little Athens, and pyramidal Cairo are left behind, and here I am writing in my room on the Ganges, in the Math. It is so quiet and still! The broad river is dancing in the bright sunshine, only now and then an occasional cargo boat breaking the silence with the splashing of the waves. It is the cold season here, but the middle of the day is warm and bright every day. It is like the winter of southern California. Everything is green and gold, and the grass is like velvet, yet the air is cold and crisp and delightful."

Swami Vivekananda disembarked in Bombay and immediately entrained for Calcutta, arriving at Belur Math late in the evening of 9 December 1900. The swami had not informed anybody of his return. The gate of the monastery was locked for the night. He heard the dinner bell, and in his eagerness to join the monks at their meal, scaled the gate. There was great rejoicing over his homecoming.

Belur Math on the Ganges

At the Math Swami Vivekananda was told about the passing away of his beloved disciple Mr. Sevier at Mayavati in the Himalayas. This was the sad news of which he had had a presentiment in Egypt. He was greatly distressed, and on 11 December wrote to Miss MacLeod: "Thus two great Englishmen [the other was Mr. Goodwin] gave up their lives for us — us, the Hindus. This is martyrdom, if anything is." Again he wrote to her on 26 December: "He was cremated on the bank of the river that flows by his Ashrama, *à la* Hindu, covered with garlands, the brahmins carrying the body and the boys chanting the Vedas. The cause has already two martyrs. It makes me love dear England and its heroic breed. The Mother is watering the plant of future India with the best blood of England. Glory unto Her!"

Advaita Ashrama, Mayavati, Himalayas (Vivekananda stayed in this house for two weeks in January 1901)

Kashmir, 1898

THE SWAMI STAYED AT THE MATH for eighteen days and left for Mayavati to see Mrs. Sevier. The distance from the railroad station to the monastery at Mayavati was sixty-five miles. He reached the monastery, however, on 3 January 1901.

The Advaita Ashrama at Mayavati had been founded with a view to enabling its members to develop their spiritual life through the practice of the nondualistic discipline. All forms of ritual and worship were strictly excluded. But some of the members, accustomed to rituals, had set apart a room as the shrine, where a picture of Sri Ramakrishna was installed and worshipped daily. One morning the swami chanced to enter this room while the worship was going on. He said nothing at that time, but in the evening severely reprimanded the inmates for violating the rules of the monastery. As he did not want to hurt their feelings too much, he did not ask them to discontinue the worship, but it was stopped by the members themselves.

One of them, however, whose heart was set on dualistic worship, asked the advice of the Holy Mother. She wrote: "Sri Ramakrishna was all Advaita and preached Advaita. Why should you not follow Advaita? All his disciples are Advaitins."

After his return to Belur Math, the swami said in the course of a conversation: "I thought of having one centre at least from which the external worship of Sri Ramakrishna would be excluded. But I found that the Old Man had already established himself even there. Well! Well!"

Group photo of Ramakrishna's disciples at Alambazar Math, 1896 (farewell to Swami Abhedananda for U S A)
Standing, left to right: *Swamis Adbhutananda, Yogananda, Abhedananda, Trigunatitananda, Turiyananda, Nirmalananda, and Niranjanananda.* Sitting, left to right: *Swamis Subodhananda, Brahmananda (on chair), and Akhandananda*

The swami and his disciple reached Calcutta from Mayavati on the morning of 24 January 1901 and in the afternoon he went to Belur Math.

The swami had been thinking of vesting the central Math with legal authority to manage the property and take care of all other matters connected with the growing organization. After considering several alternative plans, he at last decided to make a trust of the Math. Accordingly, a trust deed was executed on 30 January 1901, and registered on 6 February. By this deed, Swami Vivekananda vested all the Belur Math properties in a Board of Trustees consisting of Swamis Brahmananda, Premananda, Shivananda, Saradananda, Akhandananda, Trigunatitananda, Ramakrishnananda, Advaitananda, Subodhananda, Abhedananda, and Turiyananda — all disciples of Sri Ramakrishna.

On 17 February, which was Shivaratri day that year, the swami received M. Jules Bois at the Math. M. Bois later recorded his impressions of his visit to the swami and Belur Math in chapter eight of his French book Visions de L'Inde (Visions of India):

Vivekananda is standing on the terrace. His big eyes seemed to have eaten up his visage. This man — with almost a swarthy complexion — and dressed as the Aryans six thousand years ago — born so far from my corner of the earth — speaking another tongue and adoring another God — has been my best friend. He lived at Paris for several weeks in my residence. Together, we travelled to Constantinople, Greece, and Egypt. He incarnated for me — with his genius and his perilous frenzy — that India which I cherish as the Fatherland of my dreams — the Eden where lives the Ideal. We discussed together all the questions relating to destiny and the hereafter. Like the great Tolstoy — who is about to die — this Hindu has got the speciality that he conforms his life to his thoughts. . . .

These are the first words at the threshold of his house — "I am free, my friend — I am liberated anew. I have given all. The money weighed me down like chains. I am now the poorest man in the poorest country in the world. But the House of Ramakrishna has been built, and his spiritual family has received a shelter."

Jules Bois, a French writer
(Vivekananda stayed with him in Paris, 1900)

On 18 March 1901 in the company of a large party of his sannyasin disciples, the swami left for Dhaka, the main city of East Bengal, and arrived the next day.

There was a touching incident while the swami was at Dhaka. One day a young prostitute bedecked with jewellery came in a phaeton with her mother to see him. Jatinbabu, the host, and the disciples hesitated to admit the visitors at first. However, when the swami heard that they had come, he at once accorded them an interview. After they had saluted him and sat down, the daughter told the swami that she was suffering from asthma and begged him for some medicine to cure her. The swami expressed his sympathy and replied, "See here, mother! I too am suffering from asthma and have not been able to cure myself. I wish I could do something for you." These words, spoken with child-like simplicity and loving kindness, touched the two women as well as the others present.

Mohinimohan Das's House, Dhaka, where Vivekananda stayed in 1901

At the earnest request of the educated community of Dhaka, the swami gave a lecture on 30 March 1901 lasting an hour. Some two thousand people assembled at Jagannath College to hear him. His subject was "What Have I Learnt?" The next day he again lectured, this time on the open ground adjoining Pogose School. He spoke for about two hours on "The Religion We Are Born In." Both lectures were received with tremendous applause, and as a result of them hundreds were led to make a diligent study of his message and his plans for the regeneration of India. Here is an excerpt from the second lecture:

Shillong, 1901

This national ship of ours, ye children of the Immortals, my countrymen, has been plying for ages, carrying civilization and enriching the whole world with its inestimable treasures. For scores of shining centuries this national ship of ours has been ferrying across the ocean of life, and has taken millions of souls to the other shore, beyond all misery. But today it may have sprung a leak and got damaged, through your own fault or whatever cause it matters not. What would you, who have placed yourselves in it, do now? Would you go about cursing it and quarrelling among yourselves! Would you not all unite together and put your best efforts to stop the holes? Let us all gladly give our hearts' blood to do this; and if we fail in the attempt, let us all sink and die together, with blessings and not curses on our lips.

On 5 April the swami and his party left Dhaka for the shrine of Chandranath, about twenty-five miles north of the port of Chittagong. Afterwards they went to the famous shrine of the Divine Mother at Kamakhya, close to Guwahati in Assam. On the way they stayed for some days at Goalpara. At Guwahati he delivered three lectures. Unfortunately they were not recorded or reported; but those who heard them said: "They were brilliant. The swami was full of fire and his language was so beautiful and direct. Never before had we had such an exposition of our religion."

Both at Dhaka and at Kamakhya, the swami's health went from bad to worse. He decided to go to the delightful hill-station of Shillong, where the air is drier. It was thought that his health might improve there.

Kamakhya Temple, Guwahati, Assam

SPEAKING ABOUT HIS SHILLONG VISIT to Sharat Chandra Chakrabarty the swami said: "The Shillong hills are very beautiful. There, I met Sir Henry Cotton, the Chief Commissioner of Assam. He asked me, 'Swamiji, after travelling through Europe and America, what have you come to see here in these distant hills?' Such a good and kindhearted man as Sir Henry Cotton is rarely found. Hearing of my illness, he sent the Civil Surgeon and inquired after my health mornings and evenings. I could not do much lecturing there, because my health was very bad. . . ."

The swami's health was failing rapidly. Besides the diabetes from which he had been suffering, he had at Shillong another severe attack of asthma. During it the swami said half-dreamily, as if to himself: "What does it matter! I have given them enough for fifteen hundred years!"

Shillong, 1901 (print from damaged negative)

Shillong, 1901 (after an illness)

After the swami's return from East Bengal he lived a relaxed life in the monastery, surrounded by his pet animals: the dog Bagha, the she-goat Hansi, an antelope, a stork, several cows and sheep and ducks and geese, and a kid called Matru who was adorned with a collar of little bells, and with whom the swami ran and played like a child. The animals adored him; Matru, the little kid, who had been — so he pretended — a relation of his in a previous existence, slept in his room. When it died he grieved like a child and said to a disciple: "How strange! Whomsoever I love dies early." Before milking Hansi for his tea, he always asked her permission. Bagha, who took part in the Hindu ceremonies, went to bathe in the Ganges with the devotees on sacred occasions, as for instance when the gongs and conchs announced the end of an eclipse. He was, in a sense, the leader of the group of animals at the Math.

Old view of Belur Math

THE SWAMI'S ILLNESS WAS ON THE INCREASE. There was a condition of general dropsy. His feet especially were swollen, making it difficult for him to walk. His body became so sensitive that any but the slightest touch caused him acute pain. Sleep almost deserted him in the last year of his life. But he was resigned to the will of the Lord, and in spite of illness was ever cheerful and ready to receive people. He talked to them with his characteristic fire and eloquence, though sometimes in a somewhat subdued tone. When his disciple Sharat Chandra came to see him at this time and enquired how he was, the swami softly replied: "Why ask anymore about health, my boy? Everyday the body is getting more and more out of order. Born in Bengal, never has this body been free from disease. This province is not at all good for the health. As soon as you begin to work hard, the body, unable to bear the strain, breaks down. For the few days more that it lasts, I shall continue to work for you all and die in harness."

Buddha Temple at Buddha Gaya

I accompanied Swamiji's party to Buddha Gaya. It is not possible to describe the joy, which I feel even now. Kakuzo Okakura had come from Japan, and Swamiji went with him to show him Buddha Gaya. Miss MacLeod was with us.

Okakura had a letter from the then Viceroy, Lord Curzon, with him, and a telegram was sent in advance. As a result, at Gaya station some Government officers had come to receive the party. They very cordially welcomed the party and made arrangements for our stay at the dak bungalows [guest houses].

Swamiji went to see the Vishnu-pada-padma. Then after finishing breakfast in the morning [of 29 January 1902] all went to visit Buddha Gaya in horse carriages. We reached there about 10 to 11 a.m. The temple gate was in front of the Mahanta's [Abbot's] house. Our carriage stopped in front of it. . . . The Mahanta was then a young man of 28 to 30. He came to receive the swami along with his disciples. . . . As soon as Swamiji got down from the carriage, the Mahanta Maharaj prostrated before him. Then the whole party went inside. First Swamiji, then Miss MacLeod, Okakura, and others followed. . . .

We stayed at Buddha Gaya for about a week. Swamiji would visit the temple daily, and explain to us the architecture and the historicity of each image. In the northwest corner of the house there was an image of Buddha from Japan. The expressions on its face and mode of sitting was much like Swamiji's.

— *Naresh Chandra Ghosh*

In Varanasi the swami was offered a sum of money by the Maharaja to establish a monastery there. He accepted the offer and, on his return to Calcutta, sent Swami Shivananda to organize the work. Even before Swami Vivekananda's visit to Varanasi, several young men, under the swami's inspiration, had started a small organization for the purpose of providing destitute pilgrims with food, shelter, and medical aid. Delighted with their unselfish spirit, the swami said to them: "You have the true spirit, my boys, and you will always have my love and blessings! Go on bravely; never mind your poverty. Money will come. A great thing will grow out of it, surpassing your fondest hopes." The swami wrote the appeal which was published with the first report of the "Ramakrishna Home of Service," as the institution came to be called. In later years it became the premier institution of its kind started by the Ramakrishna Mission.

Gopallal Villa, where Vivekananda stayed in Varanasi

Kakuzo Okakura, a famous Japanese artist

Sister Nivedita and Josephine MacLeod, Bruges, Belgium, 1907

In Japan I made the acquaintance of Kakuzo Okakura who had founded the fine arts Bijitsuin school of painting in Tokyo. He was very anxious to have Swami come over and be his guest in Japan. But Swami refusing to come, Mr. Okakura accompanied me to India to meet him. One of the happy moments of my life was when after a few days at Belur, Mr. Okakura said to me rather fiercely: "Vivekananda is ours. He is an Oriental. He is not yours." Then I knew there was a real understanding between them. A day or two after, Swami said to me, "It seems as if a long-lost brother has come." Then I knew there was a real understanding between these two men. And when Swami said to him, "Will you join us?" Mr. Okakura said, "No, I haven't finished with this world yet." Which was a very wise thing. . . .

I saw Swami off and on all that year [1902]. One day in April he said, "I have nothing in the world. I haven't a penny to myself. I have given away everything that has ever been given to me." I said, "Swami, I will give you fifty dollars a month as long as you live." He thought a minute and then he said, "Can I live on that?" "Yes, O yes," I said, "but perhaps you cannot have cream." I gave him then two hundred dollars, but before the four months were passed he had gone.

At Belur Math one day, while Sister Nivedita was distributing prizes for some athletics, I was standing in Swamiji's bedroom at the Math, at the window, watching, and he said to me, *"I shall never see forty."* I, knowing he was thirty-nine, said to him, "But Swami, Buddha did not do his great work until between forty and eighty." But he said, "I delivered my message and I must go." I asked, "Why go?" and he said: "The shadow of a big tree will not let the smaller trees grow up. I must go to make room."

—Josephine MacLeod

One day the swami came downstairs and sat on the canvas cot under the mango tree in the courtyard, facing west, as he often did. His eyes were luminous; his whole frame seemed alive with some strange spiritual consciousness. Pointing to the sannyasins and brahmacharins about him, he exclaimed [to Sharat Chandra]:

"And where will you go to seek Brahman? He is immanent in all beings. Here, here is the visible Brahman! Shame on those who, disregarding the visible Brahman, set their minds on other things! Here is the Brahman before you as tangible as a fruit in your hand! Can't you see! Here — here — here is the Brahman!"

He spoke these words in such an inspiring way, that over all present there came the peace and insight of deep meditation. They stood like marble statues, so motionless and hushed in silence had they become! Swami Premananda, after his bath in the Ganges, was on his way to the shrine for worship. Hearing the words of his brother monk he fell into a state of ecstasy and became motionless. After a quarter of an hour the swami said to him, "Now go for worship." Then only did Premananda regain normal consciousness.

That scene was unforgettable. Everyone in the monastery was struck with amazement at the power of the beloved Leader who, with a word, could raise the minds of all present to the heights of the transcendental realm. . . .

Later, during his walk, Swamiji said to his disciple: "Did you see how everybody had become absorbed in divine consciousness today? These are all children of Sri Ramakrishna, so on the very hearing of the words, they experienced the truth."

Belur Math courtyard with the mango tree where Swamiji used to sit. His room on the right building upper floor faces the Ganges.

Shillong, 1901

One of the lay disciples pointed out the difficulty of establishing unity and harmony among the diverse sects in India. Vivekananda replied with irritation:

"Don't come here anymore if you think any task too difficult. Through the grace of the Lord, everything becomes easy of achievement. Your duty is to serve the poor and the distressed without distinction of caste and creed. What business have you to consider the fruits of your action? Your duty is to go on working, and everything will set itself right in time, and work by itself. My method of work is to construct, and not to destroy that which is already existing. . . . You are all intelligent boys and profess to be my disciples — tell me *what* you have done. Couldn't you give away one life for the sake of others? Let the reading of Vedanta and the practice of meditation and the like be left for the next life! Let this body go in the service of others — and then I shall know you have not come to me in vain!"

A little later he said: "After so much tapasya, austerity, I have known that the highest truth is this: 'He is present in all beings. These are all the manifested forms of Him. There is no other God to seek for! He alone is worshipping God, who serves all beings.' "

Belur Math, 19 June 1899

Sri Ramakrishna and the Divine Mother preoccupied his mind. He acted as if he were the child of the Mother or the boy playing at the feet of Sri Ramakrishna at Dakshineswar. He said, "A great tapasya and meditation has come upon me, and I am making ready for death."

His disciples and spiritual brothers were worried to see his contemplative mood. They remembered the words of Sri Ramakrishna that Naren, after his mission was completed, would merge forever into samadhi, and that he would refuse to live in his physical body if he realized who he was. A brother monk asked him one day, quite casually, "Do you know yet who you are?" The unexpected reply, "Yes, I now know!" awed into silence everyone present. No further question was asked. All remembered the story of the great nirvikalpa samadhi of Naren's youth, and how, when it was over, Sri Ramakrishna had said: "Now the Mother has shown you everything. But this realization, like the jewel locked in a box, will be hidden away from you and kept in my custody. I will keep the key with me. Only after you have fulfilled your mission on this earth will the box be unlocked, and you will know everything as you have known it now."

On Wednesday [2 July 1902] the swami fasted, following the orthodox rule: it was the eleventh day of the moon. Sister Nivedita came to the monastery to ask him some questions about her school; but he was not interested and referred her to some other swamis. He insisted, however, on serving Nivedita the noon meal. To quote the Sister's words:

Each dish, as it was offered — boiled seeds of the jackfruit, boiled potatoes, plain rice, and ice-cold milk — formed the subject of playful chat; and finally, to end the meal, he himself poured the water over the [disciple's] hands, and dried them with a towel.

"It is I who should do these things for you, Swamiji! Not you for me!" was the protest naturally offered. But his answer was startling in its solemnity — "Jesus washed the feet of his disciples!"

Something checked the answer, "But that was the last time!" as it rose to the lips, and the words remained unuttered. This was well. For here also, the last time had come.

Sister Nivedita, Calcutta, 1898

Vivekananda's room at Belur Math, where he passed away

Sister Nivedita left this graphic account: "He had spent hours of that day [4 July 1902] in formal meditation. Then he had given a long Sanskrit lesson. Finally he had taken a walk from the monastery gates to the distant high-road. On his return from this walk, the bell was ringing for evensong, and he went to his own room and sat down, facing towards the Ganges, to meditate. It was the last time. The moment was come that had been foretold by his Master from the beginning. Half an hour went by, and then, on the wings of that meditation, his spirit soared whence there could be no return, and the body was left, like a folded vesture, on the earth."

ONE DAY, ABOUT A WEEK BEFORE THE END, he bade a disciple bring him the Bengali almanac. He was seen several times on subsequent days studying the book intently, as if he was undecided about something he wanted to know. After the passing away, the brother monks and disciples realized that he had been debating about the day when he should throw away the mortal body, . . . and the day he chose of all others was the Fourth of July [American Independence Day].

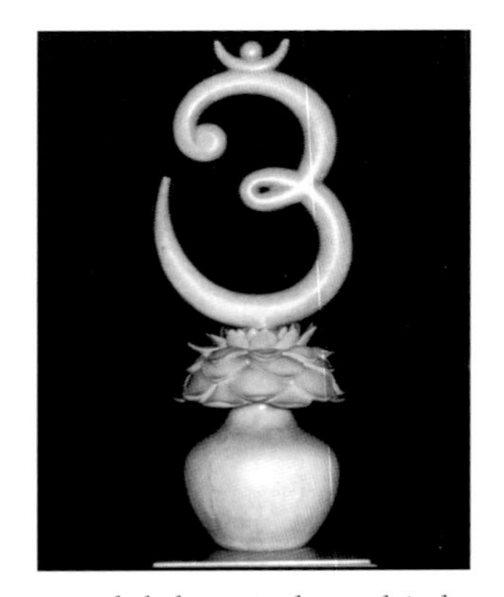

OM symbol above Vivekananda's shrine

"YOU KNOW," HE ONCE SAID TO Mrs. Hansbrough in San Francisco, "I may have to be born again." The reason he gave was not that he would have to come back with Sri Ramakrishna, as he had said at other times; rather, the will to return would be his own as well as his Master's and of a piece with his own vastness of heart. "I may have to be born again," he said, "because I have fallen in love with Man."

Vivekananda's bas-relief where his body was cremated

IN THE BEGINNING OF HIS MISSION Vivekananda wrote, "I am a voice without a form." And towards the end of his mission, he said to a Western audience: "It may be that I shall find it good to get outside of my body — to cast it off like a disused garment. But I shall not cease to work! I shall inspire men everywhere, until the world shall know that it is one with God."

Vivekananda's Temple, Belur Math

Three days before his passing away, as the swami was walking up and down on the spacious lawn of the monastery in the afternoon with Swami Premananda, he pointed to a particular spot on the bank of the Ganges, and said to his brother monk gravely, "When I give up the body, cremate it there!" On that very spot stands today a temple in his honour.

The present Belur Math from the Ganges. Left to right: Vivekananda's temple, Holy Mother's temple, Brahmananda's temple, Ramakrishna's temple, old Math building where Vivekananda lived.

The spiritual impact that has come here to Belur will last fifteen hundred years — and this will be a great university. Do not think I imagine it, I see it.

Swami Vivekananda

References

Source abbreviations are given below; for multiple quotations on a page, (a), (b), (c), etc. indicate position from left to right, top to bottom, followed by the source abbreviation and page number.

Abbr.	Title
CW	**The Complete Works of Swami Vivekananda,** Advaita Ashrama, Calcutta (Volumes: I-1970, II-1968, III-1970, IV-1966, V-1970, VI-1968, VII-1969, VIII-1964)
CWN	**The Complete Works of Sister Nivedita,** Sister Nivedita Girls' School, Calcutta (Volume I-1967)
GM	Swami Saradananda, **Sri Ramakrishna, the Great Master**, tran. by Swami Jagadananda, Ramakrishna Math, Madras (Volume II-1979)
GR	M., **The Gospel of Sri Ramakrishna**, tran. by Swami Nikhilananda, Ramakrishna-Vivekananda Center, New York (1969)
Life	His Eastern and Western Disciples, **The Life of Swami Vivekananda**, Advaita Ashrama,Calcutta (Volumes: I-1979, II-1981)
ND	Marie Louise Burke, **Swami Vivekananda in the West: New Discoveries**, Advaita Ashrama, Calcutta (Volumes: I-1983, II-1984, III-1985, IV-1986, V-1987, VI-1987)
RCI	Christopher Isherwood, **Ramakrishna and His Disciples**, Methuen & Co. Ltd., London (1965)
RV	His Eastern and Western Admirers, **Reminiscences of Swami Vivekananda**, Advaita Ashrama, Calcutta (1983)
VYN	Swami Nikhilananda, **Vivekananda: Yogas and Other Works**, Ramakrishna-Vivekananda Center, New York (1953)

Chapter I

2	Romain Rolland, *The Life of Ramakrishna*, Advaita Ashrama (1931):250-51
3	Life, I.10-11
4	(a) CW, VIII.297 (b) ND, II.239
5	RCI, 190
6	(a) RCI, 188 (b) CWN, I.251
7	(a) CW, VII.123 (b) Life, I.113
8	(a) Life, I.29 (b) CW, VII.282
9	(a) Life, I.45 (b) GM, II.831
10	(a) Life, I.107-9 (b) Life, I.48

Chapter II

12	(a) CWN, I.191 (b) RCI, 193-94
13	RCI, 194-95
14	Life, I.77-78
15	RCI, 197
16	RCI, 198-99
17	(a) GR, 730 (b) Life, I.88-93
18-19	(a) RV, 278-79 (b) Life, I.131-33
19	RCI, 206-7
20-21	Life, I.127-28
21	Life, I.162
22	(a) VYN, 33-34 (b) CW, VII.139-40
23	CW, VII.206-7
24	CW, VI.480

Chapter III

26	Life, I.193-94
27	GR, 991
29	CW, VII.248-49
30-31	(a) Life, I.214 (b) Life, I.233-34
32-33	Life, I.217-19
33	Life, I.222-23
34	(a) CW, II.198 (b) Life, I.260
35	Life, I.250
36-37	(a) Life, I.353/CW, II.403 (b) Life, I.268-70
38-39	VYN, 54-55
39	(a) CW, IV.363 (b) CW, III.139-40
40	(a) CW, VI.254 (b) VYN, 52
41	(a) Life, I.359-60 (b) Life, I.379
42	(a) VYN, 54 (b) Swami Omkarananda, *Sri Ramakrishna, Swami Vivekananda O Dharmaprasanga*, Ramakrishna-Vivekananda Ashram, Howrah (1974):127
43	VYN, 55

Chapter IV

47	Stanley Appelbaum, *The Chicago's World Fair of 1893*, Dover Publications, Inc., New York (1980): 15
48	(a) Life, I.400 (b) CW, II.230-31
50	(a) Life, I.402-3 (b) CW, V.12
51	(a) ND, I.27-28 (b) VYN, 59
52	*Vivekananda: A Biography in Pictures*, Advaita Ashrama (1966):45
53	(a) CW, V.25-26/VIII.445 (b) CW, V.100
54	RV, 131-35
55	ND, I.68-69
56	Life, I.414-15
57	(a) Life, I.415 (b) CW, I.xii
58	CW, I.3-4
59	(a) CW, V.21/ND, VI.155 (b) Life, I.428 (c) Life, I.429 (d) CW, VIII.326-27 (e) Life, I.418 (f) Life, I.428 (g) Life, I.428 (h) ND, I.87 (i) ND, I.87 (j) Life, I.428
60-61	CW, I.6-20
62-63	(a) CW, I.4-5 (b) Life, I.429
63	Life, I.427
64	(a) CW, I.24 (b) Romain Rolland, *Life of Vivekananda*, Advaita Ashrama (1931): 170

Chapter V

67	(a) CW, I.326-27/VIII.257 (b) CW, III.237-38
68	(a) CW, I.470-71 (b) CW, II.146
69	(a) CW, II.43-44 (b) CW, VII.124
70-71	CW, V.281-84
71	(a) CW, II.224-25 (b) CW, II.302-3 (c) CW, V.71-72
72	(a) CW, IV.208-10 (b) CW, I.412-15
73	CW, V.259-62
74	(a) CW, I.124 (b) CW, VIII.134
75	ND, III.106
76	(a) CW, VII.3, 103 (b) RV, 256
77	CW, VII.5, 14, 36, 44, 45, 62, 96-97, 92
78	(a) RV, 143-44 (b) CW, IV.177-78, 180-81, 183
79	(a) CW, II.177 (b) CW, II.181-82
80-81	(a) CW, VII.498 (b) RV, 171, 166 (c) CW, II.293 (d) CW, I.367, 374-75
82	(a) CW, IV.235 (b) CW, I.192-93
83	(a) CW, III.73-74, 86-89 (b) CW, VI.123-24
84	CW, II.366, 373-74

Chapter VI

86	(a) CW, VI.447-48 (b) VYN, 71-72
87	(a) Life, I.452 (b) Life, I.448/CW, VII.77
88	(a) ND, I.85-86 (b) VYN, 95
89	(a) *Pragmatism* (Longman, Green & Co., London, 1913):151-55/*Prabuddha Bharata* (March 1967):133 (b) VYN, 78
90	(a) Life, I.491-92 (b) ND, II.135/CW, VI.354-55
91	(a) CW, VIII.496/VI.420-21 (b) RV, 187-88
92	(a) ND, II.145-48 (b) From an early draft of *Late and Soon*, by Frances Leggett (Houghton Mifflin Co., Boston, 1968)
93	(a) RV, 228-29 (b) VYN, 98/ND, III.206-7
94	(a) CW, VI.366-67 (b) RV, 231-32, 235
95	(a) CW, V.101/ND, III.500 (b) ND, III.184
96	(a) RV, 258-59 (b) CW, V.101/VII.374
97	(a) CWN, I.17-18, 30 (b) CW, V.523
98	VYN, 101-2
99	Life, II.120-21 (b) RV, 294
100-101	VYN, 99-100/CW, VI.495 (b) VYN, 103
101	CW, V.104-5
102	Life, II.101-2/ND, IV.500-502

Chapter VII

105	(a) CW, IV.479-80 (b) CW, III.190-91
106	(a) VYN, 118 (b) CW, III.142
107	(a) CW, III.224-26 (b) CW, III.273-74
108	(a) RV, 77, 100-101 (b) CWN, I.164
109	(a) VYN, 121 (b) VYN, 871-72
110	(a) VYN, 122 (b) CW, VII.253-54
111	(a) VYN, 125-26 (b) CW, IV.314-15
112	(a) CW, VI.398-99 (b) CW, V.136-37
113	(a) CW, V.29/III.383 (b) CW, VII.111-12
114	(a) VYN, 139 (b) Life, II.363
115	(a) CWN, I.264 (b) CWN, I.350-51
116	(a) VYN, 144-45 (b) CW, VII.129, 131
117	RV, 233-34
118	(a) VYN, 145-46 (b) CW, III.446-47

Chapter VIII

120	(a) VYN, 150 (b) VYN, 151
121	(a) CWN, 122, 124 (b) ND, V.74
122	(a) Life, II.482 (b) ND, V.112
123	(a) CWN, I.152 (b) RV, 265-66
124	RV, 238, 266-67, 238
125	(a) RV, 265 (b) VYN, 153
126	(a) VYN, 154 (b) RV, 239-40
127	ND, V.248-49, 251, 253-54
128	ND, V.256-58, 259-60
129	(a) Life, II.502-3 (b) CW, VIII.186-87
130	(a) CW, II.363-64 (b) CW, III.536-37
131	(a) ND, V.342 (b) ND, V.327
132	RV, 364 (b) Life, II.516-17
133	(a) RV, 384-85 (b) ND, V.398-99
134-35	Life, II.512-13
135	(a) Life, II.518-19 (b) Life, II.530
136	Life, II.520-21
137	(a) Life, II.522 (b) Life, II.513
138	(a) RV, 367, 375-76 (b) ND, VI.154
139	(a) CW, VIII.504-5 (b) VYN, 155
140	ND, VI.306-8
141	(a) ND, VI.304-5 (b) ND, VI.312, 316
142-43	(a) Life, II.538-40 (b) *Prabuddha Bharata*, (March 1969):109
143	(a) VYN, 160 (b) CW, VII.378-79
144	CW, VII.379, 373, 376-77
145	RV, 260-61

Chapter IX

148	(a) VYN, 164 (b) CW, VI.440
149	(a) VYN, 164-65
150	Life, II.581-84
151	(a) Life, II.588 (b) Life, II.587-88/ CW, III.461
152	Life, II.589-90
153	(a) VYN, 167-68 (b) Life, II.603
154	(a) Life, II.622-23 (b) VYN, 170
155	RV, 241-42
156	(a) Life, II.630-31/CW, VII.234 (b) VYN, 172-73
157	VYN, 176-77
158	(a) CWN, 266 (b) VYN, 176/Life, II.648 (c) ND, VI.79 (d) CW, VI.283/V.414
159	Life, II.650
160	RV, 243

Acknowledgements

Grateful acknowledgements are made to the following for lending the photographs indicated. (The *number* refers to the page, the *letters* a, b, c, etc. indicate position from left to right, top to bottom.)

In the captions of a few photographs of Swami Vivekananda and some others, "probably" or "circa" is given when it was uncertain "where" or "when" they were taken.

To establish and focus the main theme and mood of the short, eventful life of Vivekananda, not all of his photographs could be arranged chronologically.

1. Advaita Ashrama, Calcutta: 2, 4, 5b, 6a, 7b, 8, 9, 10b, 22, 26b, 27, 28a, c, d, g, k, m, n, 29, 33b, 35b, 36a, 37, 38a&b, 39a&b, 40a, 41a&b, 43a, 57a&b, 71, 72a, 73b, 74a&b, 77b, 79a&b, 80b, 81a, 91b, 97a, 98b, 101, 104, 105a&b, 107a&b, 108a&b, 109b, 110a, 111b, 112a&b, 113a, 114a&b, 115a, 116b, 117a&b, 118a&b, 123a&b, 127a&b, 128a&b, 139b, 148a&b, 149b, 151b, 152b, 153a&b, 156b, 157a&b, 158a&c
2. Ananda Ashrama, La Crescenta, California: 140a
3. Archanalaya, Entally, Calcutta: 120a
4. Banerjee, Chaya, Bombay: 113b
5. Canadian Pacific Company, 43b
6. Chicago Historical Society: 44, 47, 48a&b, 49, 55a&b, 87b
7. Elliot Baha'i Archives, Maine: 75a&b
8. Eschner, Al, California: 5a, 7a, 145a
9. Gore, Karl, California: 78
10. Harding, Elizabeth Usha, California: 3a, 6b, 30b, 34a
11. Leggett, Frances, Stone Ridge, New York: 92b, 125b
12. Los Angeles Public Library/Security Pacific National Bank Photograph Collection: 126a
13. Mahendra Publishing House, Calcutta: v
14. Mellen, Geeta and Alvarado, Jose: 35a
15. Museum of the City of New York/H. Roger Viollet (Sarah Bernhardt acting in the role of Izeyl, January 1896): 96b
16. Nivedita Girl's School, Calcutta: 59

…hern Railway, India: 33c
18. Poetry Magazine, Chicago: 88a
19. Ramakrishna Kutir, Almora: 111a
20. Ramakrishna-Vivekananda Center, New York: 62, 72b, 76a, 95b
21. Rockefeller Archive Center, New York: 87a
22. Saito, Naomi, Japan: 155a
23. Swami Aksharananda, Dhaka: 151a
24. Swami Harshananda, Bangalore: 10a, 28o&p
25. Swami Vidyatmananda, Centre Vedantique Ramakrichna, France: 99a, 141a, 142, 143b, 144b, 150b
26. Udbodhan Office, Calcutta: 17, 23, 24, 28e, 110b, 136a
27. Vedanta Society, Berkeley, California: 46
28. Vedanta Society of Northern California, San Francisco: ii, 11, 16b, 19, 28b, f, h, i, j, l, 50a&b, 51a&b, 52a&b, 53a&b, 54a&b, 56b, 58, 73a, 76b, 80a, 81b, 83, 84, 86b, 88b, 89a&b, 90a&b, 91a, 92a, 93b, 94a&b, 95a, 96a, 97b, 98a, 99b, 100a&b, 102, 111a, 120b, 121a&b, 122b, 124a&b, 125a, 129a&b, 130a&b, 131a&b, 132a&b, 133a&b, 134a&b, 135a&b, 137a&b, 138a&b, 139a, 141b, 143a&c, 144a, 145b, 146, 149a, 150a, 155b
29. Vedanta Society of Providence: 70
30. Vedanta Society of St. Louis: 3b, 12, 13a&b, 14, 15, 16a, 18, 20, 21, 26a, 30a, 31a&b, 32, 33a, 34b, 36b, 40b, 42a&b, 56a, 61, 63, 64, 67, 77a, 82, 106, 109a, 115b, 116a, 122a, 152a, 154a&b, 156a, 158b, 159, 160
31. Vedanta Society of Southern California, Hollywood: 69, 86a, 136b, 140b
32. Viscount Margesson, Stone Ridge, New York: 93a
33. Vivekananda Vedanta Society, Chicago: 60, 66, 68a&b
34. Whitmarsh, Katharine, Santa Barbara: 75c, 126b

Chronology

1863	Mon., 12 Jan.	Birth in Calcutta
1879		Enters Presidency College
1880		Transfers to General Assembly Institution
1881	November	First meeting with Ramakrishna
1882-1886		Association with Ramakrishna
1884		Passes B. A. Examination
		Father passes away
1886	16 August	Ramakrishna passes away
	Fall	Establishes Baranagore Math
	24 Dec.	Informal vow of sannyasa at Antpur
1887	January	Formal vows of sannyasa at Baranagore Monastery
1890-1893		Travels all over India as itinerant monk
1892	24 Dec.	At Kanyakumari, South India
1893	13 Feb.	First public lecture, Secunderabad, South India
	31 May	Sails for America from Bombay
	25 July	Lands at Vancouver, Canada
	30 July	Arrives in Chicago
	August	Meets Professor John H. Wright of Harvard University
	11 Sept.	First address at Parliament of Religions, Chicago
	27 Sept.	Final address at Parliament of Religions
	20 Nov.	Begins mid-western lecture tour
1894	14 April	Begins lectures and classes on East Coast
	16 May	Speaks at Harvard University
	July-Aug.	At Green Acre Religious Conference
	November	Founds Vedanta Society of New York
1895	January	Begins classes in New York
	4-18 June	At Camp Percy, New Hampshire
	Jun.-Aug.	At Thousand Island Park, N.Y.
	Aug.-Sept.	In Paris
	Oct.-Nov.	Lectures in London
	6 Dec.	Sails for New York
1896	22-25 Mar.	Speaks at Harvard University, offered Eastern Philosophy chair
	15 April	Returns to London
	May-July	Gives classes in London
	28 May	Meets Max Müller in Oxford
	Aug.-Sept.	Tours Europe
	Oct.-Nov.	Gives classes in London
	30 Dec.	Leaves Naples for India
1897	15 January	Arrives in Colombo, Sri Lanka
	6-15 Feb.	In Madras
	19 Feb.	Arrives in Calcutta
	1 May	Establishes Ramakrishna Mission Association, Calcutta
	May-Dec.	Tours northwest India
1898	January	Returns to Calcutta
	May	Begins North India pilgrimage with Western devotees
	2 August	At Amarnath, Kashmir
	9 Dec.	Consecrates Belur Math
1899	19 March	Establishes Advaita Ashrama at Mayavati
	20 June	Leaves for second visit to West
	31 July	Arrives in London
	28 August	Arrives in New York City
	Aug.-Nov.	At Ridgely Manor, New York
	3 Dec.	Arrives in Los Angeles
1900	22 Feb.	Arrives in San Francisco
	14 April	Founds Vedanta Society in San Francisco
	June	Final classes in New York City
	26 July	Leaves for Europe
	3 August	Arrives in Paris for International Exposition
	7 Sept.	Speaks at Congress of History of Religions at Exposition
	24 Oct.	Begins tour of Vienna, Constantinople, Greece, and Cairo
	26 Nov.	Leaves for India
	9 Dec.	Arrives at Belur Math
1901	January	Visits Mayavati
	Mar.-May	Pilgrimage in East Bengal and Assam
1902	Jan.-Feb.	Visits Bodh Gaya and Varanasi
	March	Returns to Belur Math
	Fri., 4 July	Passes away

World Thinkers on Vivekananda

"The paragon of all monistic systems is the Vedanta philosophy of Hindostan, and the paragon of Vedantists was Swami Vivekananda who visited our land some years ago. . . . I have just been reading some of Vivekananda's addresses in England, which I had not seen. That man is simply a wonder for oratorical power. . . . The Swami is an honour to humanity in any case." — *William James, American philosopher*

"If you want to know India, study Vivekananda. In him everything is positive and nothing negative."
— *Rabindranath Tagore, Indian poet and Nobel prize winner (1913)*

"I have gone through his works very thoroughly, and having gone through them, the love that I had for my country became a thousandfold."
— *Mahatma Gandhi, Indian nationalist leader and social reformer*

"I was actually once put to the test of what I value most. It was in February 1939, when I had to leave Spain because of the fall of the Spanish Republic and all I could take with me was what I could carry. I chose to take one book. From the thousands of books in the library I had so lovingly built up with my father I selected *The Universal Gospel and The Life of Swami Vivekananda* by Romain Rolland. That uniquely magnificent mystical book inspired me through the years to dedicate my life to the service of others."
— *Felix Marti-Ibanez, MD newsmagazine editor and author*

"Rooted in the past and full of pride in India's prestige, Vivekananda was yet modern in his approach to life's problems and was a kind of bridge between the past of India and her present. . . . He came as a tonic to the depressed and demoralized Hindu mind and gave it self-reliance and some roots in the past." — *Jawaharlal Nehru, Indian statesman and the first prime minister of India*

"He [Vivekananda] preached to his countrymen a more virile creed than any Hindu had offered them since Vedic days."
— *Will Durant, American historian*

"His [Vivekananda's] words are great music, phrases in the style of Beethoven, stirring rhythms like the march of Handel choruses. I cannot touch these sayings of his, scattered as they are through the pages of books at thirty years' distance, without receiving a thrill through my body like an electric shock. And what shocks, what transports must have been produced when in burning words they issued from the lips of the hero!" — *Romain Rolland, French writer and Nobel prize winner(1915)*

"The most eminent of modern Indian thinkers is Vivekananda. . . . Read Vivekananda's article on God – an excellent one. Should be translated. I myself thought of this itself. . . . The book [Vivekananda's Raja Yoga] is most remarkable and I have received much instruction from it. . . . So far humanity has frequently gone backwards from the true and lofty and clear conception of the principle of life, but never surpassed it." — *Leo Tolstoy, Russian novelist and social reformer*

"If you really believe in the divine spark in man, do not for a moment hesitate to accept the great tradition which has come to us, of which Swami Vivekananda was the greatest exponent." — *S. Radhakrishnan, Indian philosopher and former President of India*